PENGUIN CANADA

UNDERSTANDING CANADIAN DEFENCE

Desmond Morton was born in Calgary in 1937. He is a graduate of the Collège militaire royal de St-Jean, the Royal Military College of Canada, the University of Oxford and the London School of Economics. He spent ten years in the Canadian Army and four years as a political organizer before he joined the history department at the University of Ottawa. He has also taught at the University of Toronto, where he was the principal of Erindale College for seven years. More recently, he was the founding director of the McGill Institute for the Study of Canada and is currently Hiram Mills Professor of History at McGill University. He is the award-winning and bestselling author of thirty-seven books on Canadian political, military and industrial relations history and a frequent columnist and radio commentator. Appointed a fellow of the Royal Society of Canada in 1985, he was named an Officer of the Order of Canada in 1996.

UNDERSTANDING CANADIAN DEFENCE

DESMOND MORTON

PENGUIN
CANADA

A Penguin/McGill Institute Book

PENGUIN CANADA

Published by the Penguin Group

Penguin Books, a division of Pearson Canada, 10 Alcorn Avenue, Toronto, Ontario,
    Canada M4V 3B2
Penguin Books Ltd, 80 Strand, London WC2R 0RL, England
Penguin Putnam Inc., 375 Hudson Street, New York, New York 10014, U.S.A.
Penguin Books Australia Ltd, 250 Camberwell Road, Camberwell, Victoria 3124, Australia
Penguin Books India (P) Ltd, 11, Community Centre, Panchsheel Park,
    New Delhi – 110 017, India
Penguin Books (NZ) Ltd, cnr Rosedale and Airborne Roads, Albany, Auckland 1310,
    New Zealand
Penguin Books (South Africa) (Pty) Ltd, 24 Sturdee Avenue, Rosebank 2196, South Africa
Penguin Books Ltd, Registered Offices: 80 Strand, London WC2R 0RL, England

First published 2003

10 9 8 7 6 5 4 3 2 1

Copyright © Desmond Morton, 2003

Author representation: Westwood Creative Artists
94 Harbord Street, Toronto, Ontario M5S 1G6

Manufactured in Canada.

NATIONAL LIBRARY OF CANADA CATALOGUING IN PUBLICATION

Morton, Desmond, 1937–
    Understanding Canadian defence / Desmond Morton.

(Understanding Canada)
Co-published by: McGill Institute.
Includes bibliographical references and index.
ISBN 0-14-100805-9

1. Canada—Defenses. 2. Canada—History, Military. 3. Canada—Military policy.
I. McGill Institute for the Study of Canada. II. Title.
III. Series: Understanding Canada (Toronto, Ont.)

FC226.M69 2003   355'.033071   C2003-901499-1
F1028.M69 2003

Visit Penguin Books' website at **www.penguin.ca**

Contents

Acknowledgements   viii
Foreword   xi

1. THREATS   1
2. MEMORIES   25
3. WORLD WARS   43
4. LAST WAR   64
5. POST-WAR   87
6. PEACE MOVEMENTS   102
7. NO LIFE LIKE IT   122
8. LIFE CYCLES   147
9. WHO'S IN CHARGE?   162
10. FUTURES   190

Glossary   214
Selected Readings   219
Index   225

To Gael

Acknowledgements

WHEN THE MCGILL INSTITUTE for the Study of Canada (MISC) opened at McGill University in the summer of 1994, it had a bolder view of its mission than some of its counterparts at other universities. An academic "institute" normally focuses on a specific area of knowledge, recruits top scholars and scientists in its field, and measures its success by the quality of their publications and by the brilliant graduate students they attract. Over its short life, MISC has attracted some remarkable scholars, from Gerald Friesen, a brilliant historian of the Canadian West, to Tina Loo, a scholar of the impact of Canadian law on the life and culture of First Nations people, to George Elliott Clarke, winner of the Governor General's prize for poetry and a humane voice for what he refers to as his "Africadian" people. We have attracted and supported some remarkable graduate students too. But our real mission was to help all Canadians to understand their country better.

This is no modest task, even with generous backing from our founder, Charles R. Bronfman, and a devoted board of trustees. The Institute has run conferences, produced videos, sent lecturers from coast to coast and maintained elaborate Web sites on a range of topics, from why we make it so hard to learn Canadian history to some of the practical ways in which we can improve our unique system of public health insurance. And, bookish people that we are, we have published books to try to help Canadians understand how their country works.

We wanted to produce books that took readers behind the simple blame games of partisan politics and the superficiality of prime-time television into real-life complexity, with a minimum of jargon. We're still at it.

Who knows where a good idea starts? Certainly it could never have happened without Cynthia Good, former president of Penguin, and a backer from the start. Looking back further, broadening understanding was a driving goal for Penguin's founder, Allen Lane. How many of us were educated by his little orange or green pocket books with that inquisitive-looking bird on the jacket?

Gerry Friesen was there early on, and his book *Understanding the West* appeared in 1996—the first title published by MISC. The next came from his fellow Winnipegger Ken Osborne. Ken is the kind of teacher all of us would want for our children. His book, *Understanding Schools*, also published in 1996, was targeted at parents bewildered by one-sided messages from school trustees, teachers, enthusiasts and critics. NDP leader Jack Layton (then a Toronto councillor) had looked hard at the old shame of homelessness, made new again in the harsh mood of the 1990s. His book, *Homelessness: The Making and Unmaking of a Crisis* (2000), presented a dose of the pragmatic idealism most Canadians have traditionally sought in public policy. The series continues. This particular book is twinned with Peter Urmetzer's *From Free Trade to Forced Trade*, another title that aims to transcend polarized rhetoric.

Writing this book has given me a fresh appreciation of all those who have kept military thought alive in Canada, and particularly in the past fifteen years. Lieutenant General Roméo Dallaire persuaded many of us to try to think some new thoughts. Doing so had not been easy or generally approved of, as Colonels Jack English and Doug Bland had discovered. Nor was it popular in universities, as Jack Granatstein, Marc Milner, David Bercuson, Terry Copp and many other friends could testify. The events of September 11 transformed my task and within a few months added several feet to my pile of reading matter. I am grateful for its authors, both acknowledged and discreet. They will forgive me, I hope, if, historian-like, I am more impressed by the continuities than any dramatic changes. I am grateful, as ever, to my colleagues at the McGill Institute for the Study of Canada, and particularly to Suzanne Aubin, who did her utmost to find me time to think and write. My McGill students, particularly those who have taken my course "The Canadian Military Experience," will recognize their questions and insights.

At Penguin, I have benefited from the wisdom, patience and imaginative understanding of unmilitary readers, from Diane Turbide and Robert Hickey to Nick Gamble, my long-suffering copy editor. As for my wife, Gael Eakin, this book would never have been finished without her patient encouragement and forbearance, and it would have been poorer without her frequent insights. Its limitations, errors and holes remain the fault solely of the author.

Foreword

I BEGAN WRITING *Understanding Canadian Defence* long before September 11, 2001, when Canada's military security issues could be found in a backwater of ill-tempered argument and obsolete impressions. Yet even in those pre–September 11 chapters, the name of Osama bin Laden appeared. Terrorism, after all, is as old as warfare. Primarily, of course, I was concerned with more classic questions of Canadian defence: Who is really threatening us? Do we have to keep up with our southern neighbour when the Americans are a superpower? Does preparing for war really make it happen?

I grew up with these questions. My great-grandfather was our first Canadian-born defence chief, though the Laurier government that appointed him always made sure that a more senior British officer was on hand. This ensured that national self-confidence never got out of hand! As an army brat during the Second World War and the Cold War, surviving five Canadian provincial education systems and a little Canadian school in Japan, I saw these questions give shape to my parents' lives and to my own. I spent eleven years in uniform, during which I graduated from Canada's military college system. In 1959, I was fortunate enough to be admitted to Oxford University, and in 1966 the London School of Economics, at a period when global defence issues were discussed with passion and insight. Then I taught in Canadian and American universities for thirty-four years. By now I have written thirty-seven books, covering political and labour history as well as Canada's military experience. Since 2002, I have been the honorary colonel of 8 Wing, Trenton, home base for Canada's air transport squadrons and for that rare but fading Canadian military capability, international deployability.

Most people who learned that I was working on a book on Canadian defence assumed that I would be in a raging bad temper at the shocking state of our military institutions. For many of them, this is a fresh discovery, while for me, it is part of my family heritage. Individuals often had their own advice on how to raise hell over the appalling state of Canada's defences. Wasn't it dreadful that we spent less on our defence than Luxembourg! Would they like to spend more? Oh, yes, certainly. How much? Estimates ranged from doubling our present defence budget to perhaps an extra billion dollars.

Sometimes my friends complained that Canada is free-loading on the United States for its security. The US Defense Department spends over $440 billion a year. Since Canada is a tenth as rich, populous and productive as the US, how about Canadians spending $40 billion a year for defence? Right now, Ottawa spends about $37 billion on *all* its expenses, from registering firearms to weeding our war memorials. Twelve billion dollars, a little short of one-third, is spent by the Department of National Defence. How would folks like to meet a real defence burden? Raising the Goods and Services Tax by one percent could bring in about $1.3 billion. Wiping out the CBC would save as much, but only after several years. In the face of such options, defence enthusiasm would wilt pretty fast.

Like medicare, business incentives, tax cuts and slot machines, defence can swallow any amount of money and keep crying for more. Understanding Canadian defence means going beyond cash consumption to trying to figure out what we should be doing and why. Ever since Confederation, there have been powerful voices demanding that we do more for our own defence and security. Yet in a long retrospect, Canada's defence policies have been brilliantly successful and, deep down, Canadians know it. In a very dangerous world, we have not been invaded, annexed or devastated. Instead, we have been allowed to play a respected role in the great world conflicts of our era. While I don't believe everything that experts tell me, I sympathize with their problems, I respect their dedication and I have learned that problems are usually more complex than they often seem to their critics.

Is Canada's era of immunity at an end? Maybe. But, as we shall see, that claim has often been made before. It has been the conclusion of all four editions of my *Military History of Canada*. Prophets, we are told, are without honour in their own land. Is that because they guessed wrong? Let's see.

1

THREATS

IN THE SUMMER OF 2001, some time before September 11, I woke up one morning to news I might have predicted. Paul Cellucci, President George W. Bush's new ambassador to Canada, had chosen an audience of American and Canadian business leaders for his first major speech. He had chosen the occasion to encourage his hosts to spend much more on defence. At just under twelve billion dollars, Canada's defence budget was about the same as it had been at the end of the Cold War, though a dollar in 1990 used to buy a lot more. In 1989, Canada kept about eighty-nine thousand people in full-time military service. Today there are only fifty-nine thousand uniformed positions in the Canadian Forces (CF). But at the end of 2001, thanks to some well-publicized problems of pay and morale, there were significantly fewer than that, with some key military and technical trades particularly low in numbers. "Doing more with less" may be a great slogan for shareholders, but over-stressed workers get sick and quit. Even more serious, for Ambassador Cellucci and his audience, much of Canada's arsenal of warships, fighters, military weapons and equipment is outdated, worn out or both. At the time of Cellucci's speech, plans for renewal were a low priority for both government and taxpayers. Indeed, polls taken in the spring of 2001 reported that Canadians knew about the sorry state of their armed forces, but spending money to improve the situation was not on their priority list.

The ambassador's message had more to do with the extent of Canada's military effort than its purpose. Under prime ministers Trudeau and Mulroney, that extent (measured as a percentage of gross domestic product) had sagged until, notoriously, it was almost on a par with that of Luxembourg, the tiniest member of the North Atlantic Treaty Organization (NATO), at 1.2 percent. Ambassador Cellucci's country, the biggest, richest superpower in history and our neighbour, spent 3 percent; France and Britain spent 2.4 and 2.3 percent respectively. Turkey topped everyone in NATO at 4 percent.

Why should we spend more? Yes, there are threats in the world—hateful dictatorships like Libya and North Korea, terrorist organizations like Hamas, Al Qaeda and the Irish Republican Army—but are they threats to Canada? Even Canadian military brass become imaginative, vague and frankly unpersuasive when asked to explain why defence should be a more urgent priority. Their favourite argument, as it always has been, is that Canada must keep up with the neighbours. But the neighbours not only have the biggest and most technologically advanced armed forces in the world, they also want to make them even bigger and better. Not even Ambassador Cellucci suggested that a greater Canadian defence effort would make his president or Congress more sensitive to Canadian or even to world opinion. Like other superpowers throughout history, Americans were going to do what they felt appropriate and Canadians could either go along or sit in the bleachers.

In early June 2001, I had been part of a briefing team put together by the Meridian International Center in Washington, DC, to help Ambassador Cellucci prepare for his Canadian assignment. Compared to most Americans, he already knew Canada well. When he was governor of Massachusetts, he had met premiers from Quebec and the Atlantic provinces. That spring, he had spent several weeks getting briefed in Ottawa.

That day in Washington, my advice was about politics, not defence. Joel Sokolsky, a political scientist from Canada's Royal Military College (RMC), shared the defence briefing with Joe Jockel of St. Lawrence University, an expert on the Canada–US air defence experience.

Sokolsky began his presentation with a characteristically shrewd, tactful and memorable observation: "Canada's defence problem is that it has no defence problem." This seems almost entirely true. Who, enjoying Washington's hospitality, could speak of an American threat—though no country in the world has as much control over Canada or so obviously wants more, from the weapons we buy to the movies we watch. So who threatens us? Many Israelis, Chinese, Pakistanis, Indians and even Australians live in unstable neighbourhoods, with real memories of being attacked. Poland, the Czech Republic and Hungary, not to mention other former members of the Warsaw Pact and the tiny Baltic states, were eager to join NATO, even at significant cost, because, within living memory, they had been overrun by the armies of, first, Adolf Hitler and then Josef Stalin.

What about us? Even in the depths of the Cold War, when Canada was the frozen filling squeezed between the United States and the Soviet Union, most Canadians most of the time ignored our awful plight. Fervent Cold Warriors and ardent peace activists provided the media with a stream of conflicting messages, but most of us went on with our lives, as we do now, without worrying that a thermonuclear exchange could reduce Canada to a smoking wasteland where, to cite a phrase of the time, "the living would envy the dead."

Today, the threat from Soviet bombers and missiles seems as long gone as the Soviet Union itself. The once-fabled Russian military machine can barely suppress Chechen rebels, much less contemplate world conquest. Russian conscripts have starved to death and their officers sell weapons and supplies on the black market to feed their families. In the West, some worry about the management and security of megatons of nuclear explosives and trillions of rems of radiation in Vladimir Putin's Russia—though not enough, apparently, to welcome their transfer and storage under Canadian auspices.

Ambassador Cellucci is not, of course, a defence expert but, as Sir Henry Wotton explained in 1651, an ambassador is "an honest man sent to lie abroad for the good of his common-wealth." The Republicans who occupy the White House and control both houses of Congress promised drastic cuts in taxes and welfare, but they also planned to spend much more on defence, particularly for high-tech weapons that might discourage even a "rogue state" from messing with the USA.

Was the ambassador meddling with our sovereignty in asking us to boost our defence spending? Some Canadians thought so: if defence enthusiasts were delighted, other citizens were grinding their teeth.

But the US ambassador was entitled to use his speech to remind Canadians of a half-forgotten but important agreement: since 1940, North American security has been a joint Canada–United States responsibility. On August 16, of that year, at Ogdensburg in upstate New York—across the St. Lawrence from Prescott, Ontario, and due south of Ottawa—Canada's prime minister, William Lyon Mackenzie King, and the United States president, Franklin Delano Roosevelt, spent several hours chatting. They then issued a press release stating that their two countries would share *permanently* in defending North America. Parliament and Congress, ministers and bureaucrats, could read about it in the papers on the next day.

At the time, virtually all Canadians rejoiced. They knew that a few weeks earlier, Hitler's panzer divisions had polished off France in a few weeks. Britain was next. Canada would then be the Third Reich's biggest enemy. We needed help. The US was still neutral and isolationist, but President Roosevelt did all he could. Politics decreed that the Ogdensburg Agreement could not mention Hitler, but what if it was permanent—whether for 1940, 1980 or the quiet summer of 2001? Done! A Permanent Joint Board of Defence met within days.

Sixty-one summers later, many Americans felt insecure. As citizens of the world's sole surviving superpower, they imagined plenty of threats, ranging from two-bit terrorists with a suitcase crammed with bottles of fatal toxins or bomb-making apparatus to psychopathic dictators in rogue states, equipped to wreak vengeful devastation on the world's richest people— and all shades of menace in between. Americans are not deeply reflective about the world. They generally see themselves as decent folks, whom any other decent people like and admire. They are astonished to discover that they or their corporate ambassadors have made enemies. Like us, most Americans believe themselves to be in the right. Accordingly, their enemies must be in the wrong. Most Canadians echo this belief. We also believe that we are so harmlessly nice that everyone must—or should—like us. Americans may feel threatened, but most Canadians find it hard even to take Osama bin Laden's warnings too seriously.

In a harsh world, power is usually based on military force. Any wannabe superpower, and some former powers that want to make a comeback, will have to humble the Americans. Anyone who thinks that is impossible should remember Vietnam.

Nice, nasty or both, great powers have a remarkably consistent history. They rise and they fall. A few generations ago, this theme made a fortune for writers like H. G. Wells and Arnold Toynbee. Enough Americans read their books about the rise and fall of civilizations to make them commercial bestsellers, but Americans nonetheless insisted that the United States was an exception. Having liberated the Philippines, they argued, the US had no empire. Having financed the Marshall Plan for European recovery in 1948, Americans were generous to a fault. Having joined the United Nations and NATO with hardly more rights than France or Britain, who could say they were pushy? True, Hollywood movies and New York publishers promoted American culture, but could you blame them if the rest of the world wanted to buy into the best way of life in the world? Dictators and intellectuals despised American values, the argument goes, but rival systems failed. Philosophical "contradictions" had killed Communism, not capitalism, in 1989.

But is any superpower immune to historical precedent? As the world's biggest power, the United States is drawn into all the world's issues, from saving whales to determining the fate of Israel. It becomes the scapegoat for anything its power and wealth might have caused, prevented or alleviated, from AIDS in Africa and Asia to dictatorship in Iraq. Superpowers make enemies and so Americans need military power. Does Canada?

Canadians have known the Americans as neighbours even longer than have the Mexicans.[1] It hasn't always been easy for either country. Canada's southern frontier was a problem even for First Nations people living north of the Great Lakes; it was the biggest challenge for successive governors of New France, until France finally abandoned its costly bid for a North American empire with the Peace of Paris in 1763. Above all, the life-and-death threat for the scattered colonies of British North America came from the south. From Champlain's encounter with the Iroquois near Lake Champlain to the last Fenian raid in 1871, the long frontier across North America was a setting for war. Armies from the south surrounded Montreal in 1760 and ended the *ancien régime*. In the fall of 1775, Quebec City was the target for two armies of American revolutionaries. Between 1812 and 1814, the Americans came closer than Canadian textbooks admit to adding most of British North America to the United States.[2]

---

1. The point can be debated, but Canada was involved in the American War of Independence, while Mexico was controlled by Spain until 1810 and the new country only experienced the full impact of US power in the disastrous 1845 war.

2. If the war had continued until 1815, the Americans would have had three battleships on Lake Ontario against one comparable British ship. Upper Canada would have fallen and, with it, the British gains in the Middle West. A British defeat on Lake Champlain ended the British advance on Plattsburgh. Exhausted after almost twenty years of war with France, the British called off the War of 1812 when they still seemed to be winning. Canada was lucky.

Between 1820 and 1840, the British spent a fortune to defend Canada. They built the citadels at Quebec and Halifax, Fort Henry at Kingston and other fortifications that now, as heritage sites, provide summer jobs for college students. Some sites, like Amherstburg and Île aux Noix, have fallen into disrepair. The British dug the Rideau Canal to resupply Upper Canada by a safer route than the St. Lawrence River. Next to India, British North America was the biggest single military headache for the nineteenth-century British Empire, and the US Civil War, between 1861 and 1865, put American military might beyond challenge. Once Abraham Lincoln mobilized the North's armies for the Civil War, British officers realized there could never be a successful replay of the War of 1812.

Confederation provided the British with a solution to a nightmarish defence threat. Manoeuvring British North American colonies into an alliance might encourage them to take on their own burden of self-defence. More certainly, it would cover a British withdrawal. No one explained this to the Canadians, least of all Colonel William Jervois, the War Office's man at the Quebec Conference in 1864, but by 1871, the last British troops had left central Canada. A British-guaranteed loan of $1.2 million to build fortifications was spent on a railway linking Rivière du Loup and Halifax. In Washington in 1871, British delegates forced Canada's prime minister, Sir John A. Macdonald, to agree to settling British–American disputes largely at Canadian expense. As later generations would discover, diplomacy in Washington was rough.

To keep a peaceful frontier, Macdonald learned to put his pride in his pocket. The Treaty of Washington was a memorable lesson in power politics. It was also the real beginning of an undefended frontier. Once Macdonald realized that the British had no intention of rescuing Canada in any future war, it became clear that Canada equally had no obligation to help Britain in its many colonial wars. Keeping peace with Washington meant keeping the border quiet. After 1868, Ottawa devoted about 2.5 percent of federal spending, a million dollars a year, to guard the old forts at Quebec and Kingston and to organize forty thousand ill-armed, poorly trained militia volunteers. It was enough to keep order in communities and along the border without alarming the neighbours.[3] Ottawa also sent a few hundred red-coated mounted police west to patrol the prairies and prevent Indian wars.

In 1898, a British general provided Canada with a defence plan, though he also urged his War Office superiors not to get involved. Canadian staff officers kept the plan up to date until 1928, when Major General Andy McNaughton ordered Defence Plan No. 1 to be burned. It had become absurd. In Washington, conquering Canada was part of an American "Plan Red"—war against Great Britain—and some such project may survive in an electronic file in the Pentagon. Outside military circles, few took such plans seriously. Who could?

In 1896, Britain and the US shared their last war scare, over Venezuela's boundary with Guyana. Too busy watching

---

3. Post-Confederation federal spending ranged from fifteen million dollars in 1868 to sixty million in 1885, the year of the Northwest Rebellion. Usually it was between forty and fifty million. The defence budget in twenty-two of the thirty-four years between Confederation and 1900 was an even million dollars. It began to rise in the Laurier years, as did inflation.

their prime minister, Sir Mackenzie Bowell, being deposed by his cabinet ministers, Canadians barely noticed. In Britain, the War Office decided to send soldiers to New York or Boston; independently, the Admiralty decided that it might only be able to blockade US ports. Neither thought of Canada. We were simply indefensible. In 1902, when Laurier hoped Britain would threaten a war to promote Canada's claim in the dispute over the Alaska boundary, Whitehall's answer was clear: no dice.

How and why Canada made a lasting peace with the United States passes unmentioned in most history books. With a firm shove from the British, Canadians found that one good way to keep the peace is not to prepare for a hopeless war. Imagine if Canadians had dutifully assumed the old British defence burden. Instead of going to school or working in farms, mines and factories, hundreds of thousands of Canadians would have spent their youth drilling and manoeuvring for a war they could never win. Ottawa would have spent millions of dollars on defence, but it could never be enough. Alarmed at military threats on their border, Americans would have mobilized armies and matched cannon for cannon. Instead, with their "peace dividend," Canadians built railways, branch plants and farms, and felt righteous about the follies of militarism.

A few other factors were involved in Canada's blessed war-free state. If the country was indefensible on its southern frontier, it was virtually invulnerable on its other three sides. The Atlantic and Pacific oceans were huge moats and, so long as Canada was allied to Britain and the US, Britain's Royal Navy and the United States Navy had no intention of letting any threat get across the Atlantic or Pacific to North America. To the north, the polar ice cap was impassable until the age of aviation, and even Canada exercised only the faintest of sovereignty over the Arctic region.

The Ogdensburg Agreement made Americans co-beneficiaries of Canada's military geography. Canadians sometimes get annoyed when Americans refer to their collection of states as "America," but when it comes to defence, the Pentagon includes Canada within the American defence shield. Why? In strategic terms, North America is hard to divide. The best place to stop any enemy assault on the United States is not on the forty-ninth parallel, Cape Cod or the Rio Grande, but far out on the Atlantic or Pacific or beyond that great frozen mass of land and water known as the Arctic. Like Franklin Delano Roosevelt in 1940, all presidents quickly learn that, as US commander-in-chief, they have to think about Canada if the US is to be better defended. No wonder Ambassador Cellucci pressed Ottawa to share more of the costs.

When the sky added a new dimension to war, most physical obstacles to a continental invasion soon dissolved. In 1914, some Canadians promoted a fantasy that wicked Germans were preparing a balloon in upstate New York to bomb Ottawa. In 1919, the first British bomber flew across the Atlantic, though it crash-landed in an Irish bog. In 1933, Mussolini despatched a squadron of the *Regia Aeronautica* to North America as evidence of his global power. In the 1930s, *Popular Mechanics* magazine claimed that the Nazis might build an airfield somewhere in Canada's Arctic as a base for a bomber assault on New York. Would Ottawa even notice?

When Franklin Delano Roosevelt visited Queen's University in Kingston in 1938, he brought a historic message:

if threatened by any other empire than the British, Canada could count on its neighbours. That promise was sealed at Ogdensburg only two years later. Without affecting Canada's war against Hitler, our home defence would henceforth be managed by a Permanent Joint Board of American and Canadian officials.

The 1940 agreement was not a free ride. Though Canada was at war and the United States, full of isolationist passion, distinctly was not, Canadians recognized their duty to American security. Ill-equipped and undertrained Canadian troops garrisoned Newfoundland, built up the major naval force in the Northeast Atlantic and flew coastal surveillance missions. When the Americans were shocked into the war by the Japanese raid on Pearl Harbor, the balance changed. After Japanese troops landed in the Aleutians and threatened Alaska, Americans poured battalions of construction workers into the North to link Edmonton to Fairbanks by road. Soon, there were far more Americans than Canadians in the Yukon and, intending no offence, they ran things their own way. Next, Americans built airfields in northern Canada that allowed US-built aircraft to reach England by stages. After 1945, Ottawa bought each of the new airfields and a by then impassable Alaska Highway.

Though during the Cold War the Soviet Union became the enemy to fear, Ottawa often seemed more nervous about the United States. Before it authorized Washington to build the Distant Early Warning (DEW) Line of radar posts across the Arctic, Ottawa extracted official recognition of Canada's Arctic sovereignty. Americans paid the lion's share of air defence costs, but the North American Air Defence Command (NORAD)—which later became the North

American *Aerospace* Defence Command—was a joint operation with a Canadian officer as deputy commander. A reluctant Pierre Elliott Trudeau and a more enthusiastic Brian
Mulroney allowed the Americans to test contour-hugging
cruise missiles on Canada's Russian-style tundra, but only
under Canadian control. Americans may have privately grum-
bled but they went along.

The Canadian–American defence partnership remains a
union of unequals. With the British, the Canadians had, over
many years, evolved an increasingly comfortable relationship.
As the stronger, more experienced partner, the British had
initially been bossy, but they came to learn that the Canadians
were volunteers in their alliance, and no longer colonials. To
ensure their co-operation, the Canadians needed to be given
autonomy. The Americans were different from the British.
While in business they were flexible, imaginative and shrewd,
their political deals were different. The checks, balances and
compromises of Washington politics left US officials with little
wiggle room to indulge their allies. Americans were generous,
imperious and always aware of their national self-interest. The
Canadians were just as sensitive about their interests.

As partner of the US since 1940, Canada has been willing
to do just enough about continental defence to ensure that
Ottawa is kept in the loop. The days of an amateur militia, the
mounted police and a handful of full-time instructors and drill
teams ended in 1940. In the early Cold War, Canada briefly
got serious about defence, devoted close to half its federal
spending to military preparedness, enlisted 120,000 men and
women, bought or built them up-to-date ships, planes and
tanks, and boasted of being first among the "middle powers."
A change of government in 1957 and a recession coincided

with cooled enthusiasm and, by 1960, defence took less than a quarter of federal spending. Under prime ministers Diefenbaker, Pearson and Trudeau, government priorities switched in favour of providing Canadians with universal health care, affordable retirement and more equal incomes.

Prime Minister Brian Mulroney was more in tune with President Ronald Reagan than his predecessor Trudeau had been. In 1984, he promised to do more for Canada's military. Three years later, Mulroney released a white paper predicting imminent Soviet aggression by land, sea and air. Instead, by 1989 Mikhail Gorbachev had called off the Cold War, Stalin's empire had dissolved and the mighty Soviet war machine turned out to be suffering from terminal rust-out. The 1987 white paper was seen as another example of Mulroney's effusive blarney, and the Canadian brass shared the blame. Wasn't "military intelligence" an oxymoron? Who could believe these guys or their pals, the growing array of defence lobbyists? For the balance of Mulroney's term and most of that of his successor, Jean Chrétien, the Department of National Defence paid for its white paper miscalculation by contributing to the war against Canada's federal deficit. By 1995, it had lost a quarter of its budget and a third of its personnel. At 0.5 percent of the country's paid labour force, Canada's full-time defenders represented an even smaller share of its workers than did Luxembourg's 0.8 percent. The US was about average for NATO at 1.5 percent.

When most of us think about Canada's armed forces going to war, our minds usually turn to the world wars of the twentieth century. But in many countries, especially in Africa and Latin America, armies seem to exist mainly to exercise power and to fight their own citizens. Soldiers are the main threat to civil society and military dictators are the norm.

That has not been Canadian experience, but Canadian soldiers have sometimes faced Canadian civilians. Few sections of the Militia Act were more consulted than those governing "aid of the civil power." Within weeks of the first volunteer units being formed in 1855, militia had fought Orange rioters in Guelph, Ontario. In 1870 and 1885, Canadian militia travelled west to the Red River and to Batoche to assert Canadian state authority against Louis Riel and his Metis followers. In 1913–14, militia occupied Nanaimo for a year to break a miners' strike. Cape Breton coal-mining towns were occupied for similar reasons in 1909–10 and again, repeatedly, in the 1920s. Magistrates summoned militia to fight strikers in Belleville in 1877, Sault Ste. Marie in 1902, Valleyfield (Quebec) in 1904, and Stratford in 1933. Militia did not go to fill sandbags or to fight forest fires or to shovel snow; they went to control and, if necessary, to shoot at crowds of fellow Canadians. Soldiers were involved in the October Crisis in 1970 and in the Oka Crisis twenty years later.

If we Canadians forget our role in foreign wars—and polls published by the Toronto-based Dominion Institute prove it annually—we also forget that our constitutional commitment to "peace, order and good government" has involved meeting domestic threats with force. Governments considered the Oka and October crises to be threats to national security, which is why they deployed armed forces to face them.[4] Canadian

---

4. Invoking the War Measures Act in 1970 was an idea that originated with the Quebec government. The municipal and provincial governments that summoned troops to uphold public order, a provincial responsibility, also had an obligation to pay for them. By invoking the War Measures Act in 1970, Ottawa relieved Quebec of the cost.

Forces' experience with international peacekeeping operations guarantees that domestic security operations are carried out with more professionalism than was possible before 1939 and more than Canadian soldiers could now bring to full-scale combat. However, few Canadians, least of all the military, relish this domestic role for our armed forces. They know from the Quebec and Oka events that, however well the job is done, short-term popularity is followed by deep and lasting resentment.

We Canadians like to think that we live in "a peaceable kingdom," able to solve even bitter arguments with calm discussion, compromise and the rule of law. If that is true, our internal threats will be small, remote and even imaginary. But are we really as good as we claim to be? How well did we respond to the Meech Lake Accord or to the Nisga'a treaty settlement in British Columbia or the Marshall decision in the Maritimes? Will we learn to accommodate six hundred self-governing First Nations? Will they accommodate a non-Aboriginal majority that plans to go on living here? Would most Canadians ever acquiesce to the peaceful separation of Quebec? In 1989, the Mulroney government changed the National Defence Act to make it easier for provinces to summon troops to aid the civil power. Now, Ottawa assumes the full costs. Recent anti-terrorism laws, allowing greater use of soldiers as police, assign those soldiers a role that most Canadians associate with military dictatorships.

Peacekeeping, beginning with Canadian truce supervision in Kashmir in 1948 and achieving an international profile with the United National Emergency Force in 1956, came to seem a wholly altruistic military role for the Canadian military. In fact, as RMC historian Sean Mahoney has illustrated, most Canadian peacekeeping contributions were intended to ease threats to allies. In 1956, NATO was threatened when American Middle East policy was undermined by the Israeli and Anglo-French invasion of Egypt. The Congo crisis in 1960 threatened to take Belgium out of NATO; peacekeeping in Cyprus helped prevent war between NATO members Greece and Turkey. Peacekeeping might be idealistic, but it also fitted Cold War needs.

Pride in Canadian peacekeeping led some Canadians to claim that peacekeeping could be a unique role for Canadian armed forces. Early in the 1990s, a "Council of 21" prominent Canadians recommended scrapping the navy and air force, enlisting unemployed youth into the army for a few years, and sending them wherever peaceful peacekeeping could be guaranteed. In equipment, training and discipline, the Council's proposed force bore an alarming resemblance to the armies that have generated so many Third World military coups. To keep armies from creating internal threats, they are best directed at external threats, growing or shrinking with the extent of the menace.

In 1993, the new Chrétien government inherited a deficit huge enough to threaten Canada's credit rating, a seemingly extravagant contract for anti-submarine helicopters, and videotaped evidence that Canadian peacekeepers had tortured and killed a Somali youth. Chrétien cancelled the helicopters, ordered a wide-ranging Somalia inquiry, and ignored the Council of 21. In 1994, amid drastic budget cuts, he promised armed forces able "to fight alongside the best against the best." Among allies, "the best" were clearly the technologically advanced Americans, but who was on the other side? Canada's clearest threat, Chrétien, his finance minister and their business backers agreed, was impending fiscal ruin. While Canadian Forces did more peacekeeping than ever, often in very dangerous places, a severely shrunken budget squeezed resources and stretched their loyalty. Unfortunately, the national finances were not part of the curriculum at military colleges, though they have shaped Canada's military history more than conventional dangers.

In the post–Cold War era, Iraq, Iran, Libya and Cuba have all worried the Americans. So has China, whenever it has threatened Taiwan. North Korea's starving dictatorship, with its million soldiers and nuclear potential, has alarmed Japan as well as its prosperous southern neighbour. Australia has grown nervous about a chaotic, corrupt and internally divided Indonesia. Canada, on the other hand, seemed remote from trouble. Doug Young, defence minister in the late 1990s, recalled a visit to the North American Aerospace Command under a mountain near Colorado Springs. The Americans were preoccupied with a North Korean "dong," or missile, which threatened to whiz as far as Hawaii. Since Canada was well out of range, Young came home unimpressed. Earlier, Brian Tobin, an ambitious fisheries minister, staged a "Turbot War" with Spain, leading the media to speculate that an obsolete Canadian submarine might someday torpedo a Spanish gunboat. Both sides sensibly preferred arbitration. A few years later, navy ships landed pathetic handfuls of Chinese refugees in British Columbia. Organized criminals used Canada's lengthy coastline as part of their system to sell cheap labour to New York sweatshops. In a well-publicized operation, a navy team seized a foreign-owned freighter chartered to bring Canadian army equipment back from the fighting in Kosovo.

Otherwise, an obscure lawsuit against the vessel's owners threatened to lock up the cargo and leave Canada's army almost weaponless. Such were Canada's high-seas adventures in the post–Cold War years.

Instead of security, prosperity and joy, the post–Cold War years even fostered nostalgia for the terrifying old superpower rivalry. Old issues of ethnic nationalism and religious fundamentalism, half-forgotten in the ideological battle of communism and capitalism, proved to be as cruel and deadly as ever. Capitalism's triumph suggested, at least in the short run, that Marx's predictions might be right: the rich grew richer and the majority of people grew poor to the point of starvation and misery. Their environments plundered for profit, poor countries faced ruin while business cruised the globe, looking for fresh opportunities for profit. Newly formed states, established in the flush of post-colonialism or the breakup of the Soviet Union, descended into civil war or anarchy. In wars of the 1990s, humans fought with little respect for the rules early twentieth-century Europe had devised to protect civilians, prisoners, the wounded and the sick. Desperation and raw hatred encouraged savagery.

While Canada was geographically remote from most such horrors, they often felt close to home because of our multicultural population, drawn from every part of the globe. From Croatia to Rwanda to Cambodia, Canadians had friends, relatives and even parents who faced destitution, torture and death. Thousands of Canadian peacekeepers came home traumatized by the horror and hatred they had witnessed and sometimes experienced first-hand. Sometimes they felt echoes in their own country—as when Canadians wrestled with Quebec or First Nation demands for sovereignty. They also recognized that their profession of arms had taken on a new and frightening relevance.

By the late 1990s, military thinkers had devised an all-purpose term for almost any imaginable threat short of traditional combat: "asymmetric warfare." Traditionally, belligerents faced enemies armed with a more or less similar array of tanks, infantry, artillery, warplanes and submarines. Asymmetric warfare was how the weak fought the strong, by ignoring the rules, hitting hard and exposing their own innocent civilians to retaliation from the powerful Western military. Should such retaliation occur, the resulting anger would generate allies for their cause. Someday historians may argue about how asymmetric war began. Antiquarians will look to Babylon; classicists will identify appropriate barbarians; post-modernists will study Michel Foucault. In the 1990s, it was the warfare of choice, waged by unarmed troublemakers disrupting a conference or crashing computer networks, by a suicidal fanatic with a garbage can bomb in Oklahoma City or by terrorists with nerve gas in the Tokyo subway system. Potentially, their "bomb" could be a nuclear device in a pickup truck or pressurized cylinders loaded with smallpox virus.

In other times, the problem of terrorists, troublemakers, computer hackers and kindred threats would have belonged to the police and security agencies. Worried governments often asked soldiers for help, but skilful police work and civilian intelligence services were usually more effective in neutralizing the threat and catching perpetrators. Blunt repression and reprisals only fed the mood of grievance. Identifying terrorists as combatants in an asymmetric war gave the military additional roles at a time when conventional "symmetric" defence challenges had become scarce. Yet asymmetric threats were as global as capitalism. In the late Cold War years, Europe had been beset by the Baader-Meinhof gang, the Red Brigades and other tiny revolutionary cells. Irish Republican Army (IRA) terrorists secured arms from Libya. Al Qaeda sheltered in the Sudan until the Taliban regime encouraged Osama bin Laden to shift his base to Afghanistan.

Setting aside professional and amateur strategists, asymmetric war began for most of us on September 11, 2001. Like the Kennedy assassination for an older generation, most of us will remember what we were doing when we first heard the news. That morning, four airliners had been hijacked. This was old hat. Everyone knew what to do: stay calm, obey the hijackers, fly to Havana or Timbuktu, and come home late but alive. This time the hijacked planes became highly effective flying bombs. The twin towers of the World Trade Center survived the impact of two airliners, but tonnes of burning aviation fuel weakened the structural steel skeleton of the buildings, causing their collapse. The three thousand victims, most of them ordinary office workers and rescue workers, some of them Canadians, had no place on any imaginable hit list. A third plane hit the Pentagon, Washington headquarters of the US Department of Defence. Outrage was loud, fully justified and, to terrorists, as predictable as the ruthless vengeance soon to be wrought on Afghanistan. Terrorists don't seek rational justice. They welcome martyrs and revel in publicity. American media gave Osama bin Laden and his followers the all-time jackpot. Al Qaeda was not newly hatched in 2001; its agents had already blown up two US embassies and the USS *Cole*. But it took 9-11 to give them world status.

There were other winners, too, though none volunteered for the contest. Calling the bombing an "act of war" by an ill-defined "axis of evil" made President George W. Bush the first national leader anywhere to invoke the NATO alliance for self-defence. Inventors of asymmetric war won some points too: they now had a palpable example. Since police and intelligence agencies had not prevented the tragedy nor nailed the conspirators, declaring war moved the US armed forces front and centre. By 10 A.M. on September 11, for the first time, NORAD had taken control of US and Canadian domestic airspace. It simply emptied the skies by grounding every civilian flight. American and Canadian interceptors were redeployed to shoot down any newly hijacked airliners. As I write, they are still waiting.

At the US Central Command headquarters in Tampa, Florida, General Tommy Franks began that day to mobilize forces for vengeance. In Halifax, Canadian warships prepared to slip their moorings and head for the Arabian Sea. At Trenton, Canadian transport aircraft began loading supplies, parts and crews. Next, they flew to a Gulf state air base, ready to broaden the American air bridge to Afghanistan. Backing an opportune civil war soon allowed the US to overthrow the Taliban regime, though it left Afghan human rights in the hands of local warlords. In December 2001, Canada joined a dirty, dangerous phase of the war by sending a seven-hundred-member infantry battalion to defend an American base at Kandahar and to fight in the hills nearby. Critics wondered why it wasn't a whole brigade of five thousand men and women. Some were upset when another Canadian battalion was not rushed to replace it—though, happily, the Canadians had not found any enemies to fight.

Back in 1914, Canada went to war because Britain went to war. The news was greeted by demonstrative patriotism in Montreal and Quebec City as much as in Toronto and Vancouver. Five years later, with sixty thousand dead and the national treasury close to bankruptcy, the mood was different. As Canada's prime minister after 1921, W. L. Mackenzie King made a fetish of proclaiming that, before Canada ever again went to war, "Parliament would decide." In 2001, as with Kosovo in 1999, NATO decided. In Parliament or outside it, Canadians had no voice.

Not that many complained. President Bush had made it plain that nations that did not side with him would be numbered among the "axis of evil." Few Canadians sided with Saddam Hussein or Slobodan Milosevic or the Taliban. Indeed the most audible complaints in Canada at the time were that Ottawa was doing too little and that Prime Minister Jean Chrétien had been outshone by Britain's Tony Blair as President Bush's top ally. Prodded by critics, Chrétien did his best to cosy up to a president he had obviously not wanted in the White House. His awkwardness in such a colonial role renewed suggestions that he was overdue for retirement.

Was Canada targeted by Al Qaeda or any other terrorists? Was Montreal's Place Ville-Marie or Toronto's T-D Centre or the George Pearkes Building, the Ottawa home of the Department of National Defence, on any Al Qaeda target list? No. Had terrorists poisoned the water in Walkerton or North Battleford? No, we managed those feats ourselves. Were we afraid for our safety? Polls said no.

But in 1914, Canada hardly featured in the Kaiser's strategy either. The only perceptible threat to Canada in 2001 came from a troubled, insecure southern neighbour, prone to the irrationality that fear produces, aggravated by media greedy for simple solutions. On September 10, national security was not a Canadian priority. On September 11, it surged up the scale.

Canadians panicked because long lines of tractor-trailers snaked back from American customs posts, carrying a week's share of Canada's exports to the States. If Canada's dominant customer kept its borders closed, Canadian workers and their bosses foresaw a grim future. Buy rockets or tanks, lock up suspicious foreigners, do whatever President Bush wants, editorials urged, so that business could do business and workers could keep working. Sitting outside Fortress America, nursing Canadian sovereignty was too hungry an option for an affluent people.

Yet had anything really changed? Since Confederation, Canadians had known the benefits of peace with the United States. We also knew that peace depended on keeping Americans secure from the north. For sixty-one years, we had managed security through a useful defence partnership. The details were forgotten but the basics were in most people's heads. Long ago Canadians had learned that when their neighbour bellows, we listen up. Then we do enough to make the elephant next door lie down again—carefully.

Which brings us back to Ambassador Cellucci. What he told his Canadian audience and its elected government is that when Americans feel really threatened, Canadians should feel threatened too. Got it?

2

MEMORIES

WITHIN A FEW YEARS, tourists in Ottawa will be invited to visit a big new Canadian War Museum on the LeBreton Flats, a former industrial site west of the Public Archives and National Library building, and south of the Ottawa River. Before it opens, tonnes of polluted soil will have been trucked away, and architects and contractors will have done their best, or their worst. Relics from the old museum on Sussex Drive or stored in a former bus garage will have been carefully selected and displayed so that visitors can follow a carefully designed and much-debated "storyline." Taxpayers will pay most of the costs of the new museum, but wealthier citizens and corporations will have their generosity amply recognized. The chief recognition though will be of the men and women who served and suffered in Canada's wars.

Those who survive to enjoy the tribute will be a shrunken crowd. By the time the new museum opens, younger veterans of Canada's last major war will be in their nineties. TV reporters will politely ask for their opinions, but what about

Canadians who wouldn't even think of showing up to see war relics? Do they care about what now seems like ancient history?

Like other forms of insurance, defence depends on experience. If we never learned that homes catch fire, that cars skid off icy roads and crash or that prized possessions disappear in the hands of unwanted intruders, who would pay the premiums for insurance coverage? Of course, not everyone has experience. Its absence in children is both endearing and frustrating. They have to learn so much that adults already know, from keeping their fingers off a hot burner to not taking candy from strangers. Teenagers feel especially immune to harm. It's why they are the first to enlist in armies. Times change, of course; experience becomes obsolete, and not all old wisdom is valid.

History is another word for experience. A new War Museum is one way to ensure that the historical fact of conflict, and the people who fought for Canada, are a prominent part of our collective experience. Like other forms of history, museums are selective. Not everything survives or was considered worth preserving. Some traditional implements of war—swords, helmets, guns, badges—are durable and convenient; others, like tanks, bombers and warships, are too bulky to preserve in quantity. A Navy submarine, planned for inclusion at an earlier museum site, is too big for the LeBreton Flats. Letters from overseas, carefully censored, were often preserved as keepsakes; letters from families in Canada turned to pulp in a rain-soaked haversack. Some parts of wartime memory, such as the smell of death or the feeling of terror, are evanescent. Reproducing them might discourage attendance.

What military memories do Canadians need now? Are any of them relevant to people living in our new century? Even to wage the new "asymmetric" war with unseen terrorists, armed forces staff officers turn to earlier conflicts to puzzle out their tactics. Generals and admirals often do fight the last war over again. How else can they know what happens when armies and navies clash? Would a crystal ball be a better guide? The past tells us a lot about wars, though it cannot tell us when another will happen, or how it will be shaped. We all learned that on September 11, 2001.[1]

What is history's lesson? You decide. If you can't know what's going to happen, why bother preparing? The superstitious or suspicious argue that getting ready for something evil helps ensure that it will happen. Or maybe you should be just a *little* prepared "just in case." Experience always leaves us choices.

There are scores of military museums in this unmilitary country. Like most local institutions, they remind Canadians

---

1. Although there had been at least half a dozen international crises in the years leading to 1914, no one predicted a war that summer (though afterwards lots of "prophets" could be heard explaining why it had been inevitable). In 1939, not even Adolf Hitler expected a second world war; he wanted it a few years later, when his Third Reich would be ready. Instead of blaming Neville Chamberlain for going to Munich in 1938 and avoiding a war, credit him with launching a war in 1939 and upsetting Nazi plans. The peace movement and the Communist parties denounced him for overreacting. No one expected the Korean War in 1950 or the Gulf War in 1990 or, for that matter, *perestroika* and the collapse of the Berlin Wall, though governments employed thousands of experts to foresee what was going to happen.

Prior to September 11, 2001, the possibility of an airliner crashing into a skyscraper *was* foreseen. As for defence against such "missiles," the joint American–Canadian air defence system obeyed orders. It looked "outward," not inward, for attackers. Those orders changed only in the light of tragic experience.

of our diversity. Some commemorate heroes like John McCrae, the Guelph-born poet who wrote "In Flanders' Fields," or Billy Bishop, the Owen Sound sharpshooter who ranks third among the world's air aces. Some museums remember navy or air force history, and one near Dartmouth commemorates naval aircraft. Nearly every regiment in the regular and reserve forces keeps a museum to remind recruits of its traditions. It works. In July 1944, after Montreal's Black Watch walked up Verrières Ridge to suffer near-annihilation, a young soldier was asked why he did it. "That's what's expected of us," he replied. He knew his Black Watch traditions.

If that seems an odd reaction from a Canadian, remember that Canada has had a very warlike history. Digging up Aboriginal burial grounds is now frowned upon, but archaeologists did enough of it to know that First Nations warriors were fighting, killing and maiming each other long before European contact. They were so intent on their struggles that, perhaps unwisely, they invited the strangers to help. Muskets and steel knives gave their owners an immediate advantage, though they turned out to be a bad bargain in the end. Europeans brought First Nations into their own wars but, once victorious, abandoned them. First Nations people were left to master new life skills on the remnants of their old lands.

Aboriginal tactics and techniques eventually shaped modern front-line warfare. Aboriginal fighters refused to stand up, form straight lines, fire volleys and die valiantly in large numbers—in short, in European terms, to "fight fair." Instead, they hid behind trees and bushes, killed stealthily and vanished until they could strike again. Europeans thought they fought dirty. A British officer, Robert Rogers, noted the techniques, trained soldiers to use them and wrote a book that started other soldiers thinking. It took centuries, but today, soldiers in any modern army wear camouflage suits, paint their faces and move silently under cover, just like Mohawk and Abenaki warriors in the eighteenth century.

Rogers's enemy, the French, learned those tactics too, though they also thought them unseemly and left them to locally born *Canadiens*, many of whom had more than a trace of Native ancestry. In their *petite guerre*, Canadian-born army officers led militia and Aboriginal allies on raids. They moved fast in any weather, struck hard and fled with booty and prisoners, while underfed French regulars of *les troupes de la marine* stayed home for garrison duty and the farm chores. Inevitably, the Canadian-born Governor Vaudreuil and European-trained generals like the Marquis de Montcalm quarrelled over strategies and tactics to save New France. Though Montcalm won a memorable victory against a British army at Carillon in 1758 and died of terrible wounds a year later, Canadian historians blame him for the fall of Quebec. They haven't been much kinder to his British opponent, General James Wolfe. The truth is that Bourbon France lacked the means to defend its colonies in the New World: sixty thousand *Canadiens* were sacrificed to European realities. *Je me souviens*, says Quebec's motto: being abandoned by France is one of Quebec's most powerful memories.

Most Canadians don't know much about the American Revolution, though it helped create their own country and transformed its population. The Quebec Act, designed to reconcile King George II's "new" Catholic subjects, infuriated Americans, who invaded Quebec in 1775. Most *Canadiens* supported neither side, but the British won and, after 1776, most of the fighting moved south. After Independence, thousands of refugees came north to start over.[2] So did Iroquois allies and German mercenaries. In fact, people kept coming to take up free land and there was no loyalty test for settlers. Living under British law, claimed Upper Canada's Governor John Simcoe, would turn them into loyal subjects.[3]

Canadians, especially Ontarians, have a better knowledge of the War of 1812, though the details are a little fuzzy. Most historians now agree that Canada was saved by the Royal Navy and a British garrison. In Upper Canada, in the crucial first year of the war, Major General Isaac Brock used a few regulars, some militia and his Aboriginal allies to smash invasion attempts at Detroit and Queenston, at the cost of his own life. After that, the Loyalists took heart, pro-Americans fled and the British sent reinforcements. The 1813 and 1814 campaigns were fought mostly by British regulars and Aboriginal allies, while the militia helped transport supplies. Once the Americans trained their own regulars, battles like Lundy's Lane were fought to a bloody draw. French-speaking regulars under Lieutenant Colonel Charles de Salaberry gave les *Canadiens* their own small victory at Chateauguay in 1813. This memory became useful in later years whenever bigots claimed that French Canadians would not fight for Canada.

---

2. Among them were my mother's ancestors from New York. Captain Nathaniel Frink had the joy of being aide de camp to Benedict Arnold, the Revolution's best general and the United States's best-known traitor. Arnold wasn't popular here, either, and soon left for England.

3. Georgeville, the village where I spent last summer, began life as Copp's Ferry, founded by Moses Copp as a terminus for his horse-powered ferry across Lake Memphrémagog. The Daughters of the American Revolution sent a plaque to help us remember that Copp was a captain on the winning side.

The War of 1812 created many myths, some of them even true. Profits from privateering and supplying the Royal Navy taught Maritimers that war was a good way to get rich. Customs revenues collected while Britain controlled Maine started Dalhousie University. Just as useful was a myth that raw militia had saved Upper Canada. Myths may be true or false but they always serve a purpose. Politicians ignored old British regulars but militia veterans and their friends had votes. Flattery brought applause. Besides, if untrained militia with their own shotguns could beat off an enemy, why raise taxes to arm and train "real" soldiers? The "militia myth" was useful enough to last a century.

Canada's colonial masters knew better. In the world as seen from Whitehall, Canada ranked just after India's frontier with Afghanistan as Britain's biggest defence problem. British taxpayers spent a fortune on building the canals and forts needed for another War of 1812. In the 1840s, they stopped. Even efforts to organize the militia faded. Empire went out of fashion. After the British redeployed their soldiers to the Crimean War in 1855–56 and the Indian Mutiny in 1857–58, the Canadas reluctantly created a five-thousand-member "volunteer militia" for a few years. When Queen Victoria's son, the Prince of Wales, visited North America, volunteer militia everywhere got a second wind. How better to get a close look at the Prince than by forming a guard of honour or guarding the streets where his carriage passed?

In 1914, Americans, the British and (belatedly) Canadians planned to celebrate one hundred years of an undefended, peaceful border. This was, perhaps, half true. After 1814, regular threats of war had rattled the Canadian border, often in presidential election years. Some of the most serious came in the 1860s. To distract Americans from fighting each other over states' rights and slavery, Lincoln's secretary of state, William Seward, suggested that the US could go to war with Britain, seize Canada and substitute its three million people for the three million southerners in the Confederate States. When a US frigate stopped a British mail steamer and removed two Confederate officials, war was imminent.

Britain promptly despatched every soldier it could spare; Nova Scotia revived its old militia and New Brunswick enrolled volunteers. In Canada, the government announced militia reform, only to be defeated in a partisan manoeuvre. Outraged by the ungrateful and heedless colonials, Whitehall soon found a better argument for not fighting another War of 1812. American generals bumbled, contractors robbed and soldiers forgot to salute, but Lincoln's army impressed British observers. If the Americans invaded Canada, they would win—easily. If war came, the British would be wise not to be there.

There were lots of arguments for Canada's Confederation in 1867, from providing a common market for colonial products to promoting western expansion. In 1865, Canadian politicians promised to spend a million dollars on defence in return for a British pledge to defend the new country. Colonel W. F. D. Jervois, the British Army's observer at the Confederation negotiations, assured colonial politicians that they could easily defend themselves, without spilling the beans—that they would soon have to do so on their own. Post–Civil War raids on Canada by "Fenians," armed Irish veterans of the American war, encouraged militia rearmament and training. When the Fenians fled, Canadian self-confidence soared. Who cared when the British announced their withdrawal in

1868? After managing a tricky expedition to the Red River, the last British troops left Quebec City on November 11, 1871.[4] By then, British diplomats had wiped clean the slate of outstanding Anglo-American disputes in the Treaty of Washington, often at Canada's expense. The future US relationship was largely up to Canadians.

Ottawa refused to panic. Confederation-era politicians had grasped a truth that had eluded the British: so long as Americans felt their northern boundary was secure, they would not attack. A new Militia Act in 1868 showed Canadians what a million dollars would buy: forty thousand volunteer militia members, as efficient as forty-eight evenings of training or two weeks in camp over three years could make them.[5] The new militia could cope with disorder; going to war was another matter. Americans could sleep easy.

The militia minister, Sir George-Étienne Cartier, enlisted some artillery to take over abandoned forts at Kingston and Quebec. A tiny staff, usually chosen for party loyalty, organized local units and presided over training camps. Sham

---

4. Troops remained at Halifax, a British naval base, and returned to Esquimalt in the 1890s. In 1896, the US and Britain drifted close to war and American officers planned to invade Canada. The British made no real plans to stop them. The Army considered landing a force at Boston and New York and making "offensive gestures"; the Royal Navy doubted it could defeat the US fleet.

5. A "volunteer" militia seemed a contradiction in terms to many Canadians. Even in 1868, almost every fit Canadian male belonged to the "reserve militia." Letting some volunteer to serve had seemed a dangerous innovation in 1855 and again in 1868. Sir George-Étienne Cartier stuck to the principle: unless service was a matter of choice in Canada, the militia would wither and die. In Quebec, where red coats and British traditions had little appeal, the militia grew very weak. Elsewhere, imitating Queen Victoria's army was highly popular.

battles pretended to drive back American invaders; the militia's real purpose was to nip riots in the bud. As Mexico was learning, nothing invited American invasion faster than a disorderly border. When whiskey traders provoked violence in the West, Ottawa sent three hundred red-coated police to forestall the US cavalry. If Yankee politicians "twisted the British lion's tail" in election years, Canadians had lived with it all their lives. In fact, Canada owes its founding politicians much for their cool response to the American threat. By treating its oldest and closest enemy as a friend, Canada could instead build its economy. Canada's European "parents," Britain and France, gained too. In both of the great twentieth-century wars, Canada felt secure enough to send virtually its whole armed forces to defend its old imperial protectors.

To be fair, some Canadians feared they might need the British. Despite budget crises, they kept close to their million-dollar pledge for defence, though as the years passed it bought less and less. Between 1874 and 1920, the Canadian militia was overseen by a British officer under various titles. When Prime Minister Alexander Mackenzie opened the Royal Military College of Canada in 1876, he modelled it on the US Military Academy at West Point, but its top graduates became British army officers. Few graduates hoped for Canadian military careers; many became civil engineers.

Canada's militia was the first line of defence in a war that could not be allowed to happen. Obliged to spend money on camps, uniforms, pay and armouries, successive Liberal and Tory governments demanded political rewards. Ministers promoted friends, chose suppliers from party patronage lists and located camps near friendly communities. British barracks and a fort helped Kingston become a military base, as did its

MP, Sir John A. Macdonald. When Laurier's government approved the new Ross rifle in 1902, the factory was built in Sir Wilfrid's Quebec East riding. As the few hundred artillery of 1872 became a "Permanent Force" (PF) of almost a thousand, officers' commissions became patronage plums for sons of party supporters. In 1867, a quarter of the MPs were also senior militia officers: a battalion of three hundred militia constituted a useful political machine. "Colonel's Day," as the annual parliamentary defence debate was called, reflected their concerns: camps, uniforms and any evidence that the British general or his Canadian staff were putting on airs as "regulahs" and being snooty to Canada's real defenders, the militia.

In Queen Victoria's Canada, rural militia pitched their tents, drilled, fired a few shots from elderly rifles and rehearsed for the grand review or sham battle that climaxed their time in camp. Drink and conviviality filled the evenings. Volunteers joined for three years; one camp was usually enough. Sweat-soaked uniforms were passed to the next recruit. City battalions trained at their local armouries and attracted recruits by being active social and athletic clubs. Officers paid for elaborate dress uniforms, supported their own mess and paid a rich subscription to buy instruments for the band and outings for the lower ranks. Being a militia officer, especially in a "smart" city regiment, was not for the riff-raff. (Nor was imitating the British aristocracy interesting to most French Canadians. Montreal had only two French-speaking regiments, along with six of the richest English-speaking units in Canada.)

British observers rated only the field artillery as efficient. Did it matter? The militia coped easily with strikes, riots and, thanks to Louis Riel's inept leadership, the 1885 campaign in the North West.[6] Occasionally, it improved. Dr Fred Borden, a militia surgeon from Nova Scotia, became Laurier's minister of militia in 1896. He helped create a medical corps, a signal corps, an army service corps to organize transport and supplies, and an ordnance corps to store weapons, equipment and clothing. He appointed military nurses and insisted that they be commissioned as officers. Since reliable maps had yet to be drawn and Canada's defenders would need guides to keep them from getting hopelessly lost, Borden even approved a Corps of Guides. Canada's militia, Borden believed, must be a complete army, not a few fighting units attached to someone else's army. Remembering 1896, when the Venezuela crisis had brought war with the United States very close, Borden insisted on a plan for such a war. In various versions, Defence Plan No. 1 lasted into the 1920s.

Meanwhile, Canada's military scene would shift.

In the past, some Canadians had joined the British services. One was Lieutenant James Dunn, who won a Victoria Cross for his role in the famous charge of the Light Brigade. When

---

6. Riel refused to allow his lieutenant, Gabriel Dumont, to launch night attacks, which might well have panicked the raw militia. "Too barbarous," he said. The Canadians were well served by their elderly British commander, Major General Fred Middleton. He stayed awake most nights, checking on sentries. He recruited local scouts, who spotted Dumont's ambush at Fish Creek. Middleton ignored pleas from frightened prairie towns and focused on Riel's headquarters at Batoche—when Riel foolishly stayed to fight him. By providing the logistics system the militia utterly lacked, the Hudson's Bay Company made the campaign possible—a fact that, in later years, the company preferred not to publicize.

Dunn raised the 100th Regiment (Royal Canadians) in 1856, hundreds of Canadians joined. In 1857, during the Indian Mutiny, another VC winner was William Hall, a black Nova Scotian in the Royal Navy. Whenever the British were on the verge of war, militia colonels and captains offered themselves and their men. Top RMC graduates joined the British army.[7] When Major P. O. J. Hébert, an artillery officer attached to the British Army, died of malaria in Cairo in 1881, he became the first Canadian soldier to die on active service overseas. In 1885, Canadian boatmen helped transport a British force up the cataracts of the Nile, too late to save Victorian hero Major General Charles Gordon. Thirteen years later, Colonel Percy Girouard, a Montrealer and RMC graduate, built railways that bypassed the Nile and took the British to Khartoum. Other young Canadians died in West Africa as British officers, fighting slave traders and fever.

In the late 1800s, most Canadians had British roots; many identified with an Empire that spanned the world. Some, like colonels George T. Denison and Sam Hughes, insisted that Canadians were tougher and brighter than the English and, someday, would inherit the Empire. When Britain went to war against two Boer republics in September 1899, a media campaign inspired by Montreal's Hugh Graham pressed for Canada to offer troops. Colonel Hughes announced that he would lead a contingent. Anxious only for an official

---

7. Those with no means or political "pull" settled for the North West Mounted Police (NWMP). One such was Aylesworth Bowen Perry. Perry had accepted a British commission but his father lost his fortune. Though he was a Liberal, kindly Tories stretched a point, and Perry became an NWMP Inspector. Delighted to find a Grit in the force, the Laurier government helped his career. Perry, needless to say, had talent too!

commitment, the British had him squelched. Canada was deeply divided. Some echoed Graham; others insisted that the war was none of Canada's business. Debate was passionate. The government split. A reluctant Laurier felt Ontario votes slipping away. On October 15, he spoke: a thousand Canadians would go. English-language media cheered. Within two weeks, a thousand-member battalion had been recruited and organized and had embarked on a steamer at Quebec— fast work even by today's standards.

In Ottawa, Laurier insisted that sending a few troops was too minor a decision to have MPs ratify. His sharpest critic, Henri Bourassa, insisted that a dangerous precedent had been set. Laurier denied it. Bourassa was right: South Africa set the pattern for 1914, 1939 and 1950.

In South Africa, British generals fumbled badly but Canadians appeared to fight well under their own officers. Laurier had suggested breaking up the unit in South Africa, and it was designed to be split in two. The Governor General, Lord Minto, fought for unity—anything else, he said, would be "undignified." Lieutenant Colonel W. D. Otter, aged fifty-nine and a veteran of the Fenian Raids and 1885, trained his battalion and led it in battle, surviving a bullet in his neck and face to complete the year-long campaign. His second-in-command and many subordinates resented Otter's discipline, but one precedent was set: Canadian soldiers would fight as Canadians. In February 1900, Canadians even got credit for winning the Battle of Paardeberg.[8] A second contingent of

---

8. On February 26th, Canadians staged a night attack on the Boer camp. It failed, but two companies from the Maritimes did not hear the order to withdraw. The Boers had already decided to give up on the 27th. When dawn broke and white flags appeared, the Canadians got the credit.

Canadian mounted rifles proved such a match for Boer farmers that the British themselves recruited more. By war's end, thousands of Canadians had served. Some, like Sam Hughes, declared that the British had nothing to teach Canadians about soldiering; a few realized that both they and the British had a lot to learn. Canadian officers came home with new experience and prestige. Stung by their failures, the British launched major reforms, including a new general staff and better weapons.

European hostility during the war, and American sympathy for the British, also changed the diplomatic equation. It was less likely than ever that Britain would back Canada in its dispute over the Alaska boundary. A united Germany, once a British ally, had become a dangerous threat on land and at sea. To concentrate its fleet in home waters, the Royal Navy abandoned far-flung commitments, including its bases in Esquimalt and Halifax. As the British army began preparing for a European war, officers began the discreet conversations with French counterparts that would lead to the Western Front in 1914. Part of the planning included integrating the colonial troops who had proved so useful against the Boers. Common training, equipment and doctrine would make them even more useful.

Canadians had little grasp of the implications, but the newly prosperous country could now afford to spend on defence. Laurier expanded the Permanent Force to garrison Esquimalt and Halifax. The United States remained the official enemy, but Boer War experience argued for modern weapons and serious training. If Britain again fought a major war, Canadians would be there; South Africa *was* a precedent.

In British Columbia, perceptions of threat were different. Isolated between the Pacific and the Rockies, a few hundred thousand white settlers felt chronically endangered, both by Aboriginal people who outnumbered them and by hundreds of millions of Asians suddenly endowed with military power when Japan defeated Russia in 1905. British Columbia was far from Ottawa and it spoke with many voices, from respectable, wealthy conservatives to the first elected socialists in the British Empire. Employers argued that cheap Asian labour would build a prosperous West Coast economy, but most British Columbians shivered at the "Yellow Peril" and wondered whether Britain's shrinking Pacific fleet would still protect them.

In the 1900s, militarism was fashionable in Canada. A Canadian Defence League linked professors, bishops and leading businessmen, along with militia colonels, to urge compulsory military training for men and cadet corps for boys.[9] By 1910, Fred Borden, Laurier's defence minister, had helped make school cadets compulsory in all provinces but Saskatchewan.[10]

In the face of such activity, opponents of imperialism made themselves heard. Peace was a popular moral cause, linked with Prohibition, votes for women and a Protestant social gospel that promoted the brotherhood of man worldwide as

---

9. Sam Hughes's brother James, chief inspector of Toronto's schools, established cadet corps for the city's boys and, as a feminist and suffragist, insisted on training girls, too.

10. Borden and Sam Hughes both resented British generals. Borden's son Harold had died in action in South Africa. In vain, his grieving father demanded a posthumous Victoria Cross for him. Hughes, who shared his South African exploits with Canadian newspapers, also wanted a VC—for himself. Instead, the British sent him home for belittling his superiors in Cape Town newspapers. In 1915, the British promoted him to lieutenant general—but still no VC!

well as in the nearby slums. Laurier himself warned Canadians not to be sucked into "the vortex of European militarism." Even military enthusiasts were conservative. When Canada's air pioneer, F. B. McCurdy, displayed a military version of his *Silver Dart*, politicians and generals agreed that Canada had no need for "aerodromes."

In Toronto, a Navy League urged the creation of a Canadian-owned fleet. Still angry that Britain had not risked war for Canada's claims to the Alaska panhandle, Laurier agreed. In 1909, a small naval college opened at Halifax and in 1910 the acquisition of two aging British cruisers launched the Royal Canadian Navy (RCN). The British would have preferred a Canadian cash donation to support the Royal Navy; so did the Opposition Tories, once their imperial duty was explained to them. They also noted that, thanks to Henri Bourassa and his *nationalistes*, the new navy had sparked outrage in Quebec. Warships, flying the British white ensign, would involve Canada in any British war. In 1911, imperialists and *nationalistes* united to defeat the Liberals. Laurier was scuttled, although his navy proved harder to sink.

To replace him, Canadians chose a dull, dogged Nova Scotian, Robert L. Borden, as their new prime minister. Sam Hughes, a faithful backer in party battles, expected to be minister of militia. Nervously, Borden agreed. Neither before nor since has Canada had a militarist as defence minister. Provided that booze was banned—Sam was a prohibitionist too—he believed military life was good for men. Since he was also a feminist, he thought it might even be good for women. The Boer War persuaded Hughes that a soldier needed only to know how "to pink the enemy every time." By 1911, most

Tories knew that the Canadian-made Ross rifle, adopted in 1902, was a big Liberal mistake. Hughes was its devout defender. As minister, he built scores of armouries, expanded the militia to sixty thousand men and forced city regiments to go to camp. He cut the Permanent Force, and militia officers grinned when Sam denounced PF officers as "barroom loafers." On the eve of the First World War, the weaknesses of Canada's militia were enormous but it was probably as well prepared for war as it could be, given Canada's militia myth and the corresponding contempt for military professionalism.

Laurier's navy suffered a different fate. The Borden government cancelled recruiting and instead proposed that Canada pay for four new "Dreadnought" battleships for the Royal Navy. Liberal senators defeated the proposal, over-expansion of railways helped collapse the Canadian economy, unemployment reached fifteen percent and Borden put his naval policy aside. War in 1914 seemed highly unlikely. Hard times made "Drill Hall Sam" Hughes less popular. The government belatedly discovered that prominent people in Britain and the United States were planning to celebrate a hundred years of peace, and invited itself to the party. And then some Balkan terrorist shot an Austrian archduke.

3

WORLD WARS

Dᴜʀɪɴɢ ᴛʜᴇ 1991 ɢᴜʟғ ᴡᴀʀ, I was principal of the University of Toronto's campus in the very multi-ethnic Mississauga. One day, soon after the bombing of Baghdad began, a delegation of Iraqi students arrived. "How could our country, Canada, be bombing our country, Iraq?" they demanded. A precise, factual answer was that Canada's 416 "Desert Cat" Squadron was distinctly *not* bombing anything at the time and would finish the war claiming only a "possible" hit on a very small Iraqi gunboat. Instead, I heard out their message, noting how one of the young men had told me earlier how his father had narrowly escaped torture and death at the hands of Saddam Hussein. In fact, like most sensible people, the student easily distinguished between the bombing of a great city and its population, and the punishment of its villainous ruler. Most Canadians come from somewhere else. Trudeau-era multiculturalism policies ensure that we are not very pushy about it, but most of us assume that, in due course, newcomers will indeed become Canadians. We must also acknowledge that it takes a while. Meanwhile, like the Iraqi students, many of us still carry strong homeland loyalties that have nothing to do with current politics. For coalition flyers to bomb Baghdad, a historic metropolis of Arab culture, was as much a sacrilege as Hitler's Luftwaffe bombing London or laying explosives to demolish Paris in 1944.

Canada was not significantly threatened by Germany in the two world wars, but the ancestral homelands of its two largest ethnic components were, and the most plausible explanation of why Canada entered both world wars is our pre-existing loyalty. It gripped William Lyon Mackenzie King in 1939 as surely as it controlled Sir Robert Laird Borden a quarter-century earlier. Such loyalty burned lower in longer-settled parts of English-speaking Canada and was all but extinguished for most *Canadiens*.[1]

Since 1945, Canada's ethnic diversity has exploded. Every part of the world is represented here, and multiculturalism has helped cultural and national communities to gain a voice. As in the world wars, people feel entitled to have their divided loyalties reinforce each other even—and perhaps especially— when war is involved. When the loyalties conflict, as they did for my Iraqi students, or for many Serbs in 1999, the emotions are bitter and, to other Canadians, perhaps unexpected.

By early 1914, Colonel Sam Hughes's warnings of imminent war sounded absurd. In March, the militaristic Canadian Defence League folded. Borden spent his summer holiday pondering whether to dump his defence minister. On the hot

---

1. Few in Quebec besides Henri Bourassa's former young tiger, Olivar Asselin, consciously raised soldiers by appealing to loyalty for France. Of course, the Third Republic had angered Catholics in France and Quebec by imposing secular schools.

August holiday weekend, Sam Hughes sulked in his office. The British, he feared, would "skunk it." He commanded that the Union Jack that flew over militia headquarters be hauled down.

Early on August 4, news that Berlin had dismissed a British demand to withdraw from Belgium brought rejoicing echoing from crowds from Halifax and Quebec City all the way to Vancouver. At once, Hughes scrapped a three-year-old mobilization plan and telegraphed two hundred militia colonels to bring volunteers to Valcartier, outside Quebec City. Next he ordered an old pal, Colonel William Price, to build a camp, and the biggest rifle range anywhere. Sir Robert Borden summoned the cabinet to approve a twenty-five-thousand-member Canadian contingent. When thirty-three thousand volunteers had appeared by mid-September, a weeping Hughes persuaded the cabinet to send them all overseas.

Valcartier was a dusty sea of confusion, with a red-faced, swearing Colonel Hughes in full command. He formed and re-formed battalions, promoted and demoted officers and jumped from his horse to demonstrate drill movements. Harried staff fielded abuse and struggled to keep order. Any married man lacking his wife's permission to enlist went home. At the end of September, Colonel Price loaded horses, wagons, guns, equipment and men into thirty ships. Military professionals were aghast: the contingent was untrained, poorly equipped and disorganized. French Canadians were split in three different units. Civilians thought Valcartier a miracle and a model of how a democratic army should be run. Borden, who quietly agreed with the professionals, yielded to the public view.

The official plan would have based the contingent on some militia units and thereby enraged the others. Hughes's method avoided a storm, though some battalions identified with militia parents like Montreal's Black Watch, Winnipeg's "Little Black Devils" or Toronto's 48th Highlanders. Eventually, local militia regiments helped organize most of the 262 infantry battalions ultimately created for the Canadian Expeditionary Force (CEF), but Hughes had made it hard to link the peacetime militia to Canada's wartime army.[2] Still, a million men (out of eight million Canadians) volunteered and over half of them ultimately became soldiers.

Across the Atlantic, most of the mess was cleaned up. On Salisbury Plain, under the pelting rain of the wettest winter England could remember, the contingent became the 1st Canadian Division. A British general took command. The worst officers were sent home and much useless equipment was scrapped, from cardboard-lined "sham shoes" to the McAdam "shield-shovels" that Hughes dreamed of pushing all the way to Berlin. The Ross rifle would have vanished too, if the British had had enough rifles to replace it.[3] In February 1915, the Canadians went to France. After a cautious introduction to trench fighting, the Canadian Division moved up

---

2. Some links were embarrassing. Militia weakness in Quebec damaged recruiting. Colonel Arthur Currie of Victoria took money intended to pay for his militia regiment's Highland uniforms and applied it to his personal debts. In 1917, he pressured rich subordinates to help him pay back the money, and cabinet ministers hushed up the scandal.

3. The Ross was accurate, but long and heavy. Its straight-pull bolt action gave no leverage to help remove a spent cartridge. Worse, since the British Army's inch was a little bigger than everyone else's, cartridges tended to jam in the breach, making rapid fire difficult. Imagine how troops facing a German mass attack felt. Hughes fired the Division's first commander for condemning the Ross but, by the summer of 1916, it was replaced. The Ross helped arm British Home Guards in 1940, and served Canadians as a sniper rifle in Korea in 1951.

the line to a place called Ypres. Months earlier, much of the British regular army had died there, stopping the last German offensive of 1914. Ypres was a small remnant of Belgium but, to British generals who had lost sons and friends, it was sacred ground. It was also sodden from rain, and the trenches were shallow and ill-protected. There, in the fourth week of April 1915, Canadians fought their first major battle in history.

Second Ypres, as it was called, was a minor German offensive on weak Allied defences, a diversion while their main army tried to knock Czarist Russia out of the war. It was also a chance to try out an illegal "secret weapon," chlorine gas. On April 22, 1915, it worked well. The green choking cloud dissolved two French divisions so fast that the Germans could not catch up. Canadians were worried too, but that night they covered their flank with a counterattack, while the British sent help. On the third day, April 24, it was the Canadians' turn. By nightfall, German artillery, gas and bayonets had forced the survivors back to their reserve lines. Ill-coordinated counterattacks, British and Canadian, held the line but no more. When the division was relieved, 6,035 men—a third of its members—were killed, wounded or captured.[4]

Was Second Ypres a defeat? Key ground was given up. The divisional commander had exercised little leadership; one brigadier hid in his dugout; another went back to seek help instead of sending a messenger. The elderly colonel of a shattered battalion showed up drunk in Boulogne. Wisely, the

---

4. Communiques were discreet about the 2,000 Canadian prisoners because home audiences were told that Canadians "fought to the death." The casualty report for April 1915 listed 3 of 6,035 casualties as dead from poison gas. In the 2 French divisions that first encountered chlorine gas, official reports listed 5 dead. Most of the victims were left in German hands.

British commander, Field Marshal Sir John French, recognized that raw troops had done better than anyone had a right to expect. Instead of casting blame, he proclaimed that the Canadians had "saved the situation." Chlorine gas was the alibi for losing ground. Heroes collected Victoria Crosses. Colonel John McCrae's poem, recited on countless Remembrance Days since, appeared in *Punch* as a cry for vengeance. Officers who survived Ypres, even those who made mistakes—Currie, Turner, Mercer, Lipsett, Watson, Burstall—went on to lead the Canadian Expeditionary Force. By war's end, almost every senior commander in the Canadian Corps was a veteran of Second Ypres. Even the drunken colonel went home with a promotion. He just happened to be an MP.

Soon more divisions arrived to form a Canadian Corps. The 2nd Division came from Canada, the 3rd was created in France and a 4th Division was organized in England. Thanks to inexperienced generals and staff, limited tactics and amateurishness against a very professional enemy, each division experienced a disastrous introduction to battle. At a cost of thousands of lives, each division learned its business; some learned it better than others. During the freezing winter of 1916–17, the Canadian Corps figured out some of the lessons of the 1916 Battle of the Somme and, on April 9, 1917, applied them to capture Vimy Ridge. Artillery located and destroyed enemy guns; then they crushed German fortifications. Engineers dug tunnels that took soldiers closer to enemy lines. Staff compiled every scrap of information and trusted junior leaders to use it. Infantry attacked in mutually supporting teams, not in line. At a cost of ten thousand dead and wounded, Canadians delivered the first real Allied victory on the Western Front. Doing great things together, said the French philosopher Ernest Renan, is how nations are formed. Vimy was such a moment.

The Canadians were not unique in either courage or tactics, but they fought as a single team, designed by a sensible British general, Sir Julian Byng. His model was adapted and improved after May 1917, by a pear-shaped businessman from Victoria, Lieutenant General Sir Arthur Currie. Personnel shortages forced the British and Australians to weaken their divisions; Currie made his bigger, adding artillery, machine guns and a whole brigade of engineers. By August 1918, the Canadian Corps packed the punch of a small army. Currie's staff learned to integrate their resources until, in a hundred days of attacks, from August to November 1918, the Canadian Corps broke every German line and took every objective it was assigned. Instead of ending in 1920, as the best-informed Allied experts had predicted, the end came on November 11, 1918.

"If you need their men," an advisor warned the British prime minister, "you must call them to your councils." On the strength of the Canadian Corps, Borden joined other Dominion prime ministers as decision makers in the Empire's war and, at the peace negotiations at Versailles in 1919, Canada took its first tiny step on the world stage. Canada had begun the war as a patriotic colony; it emerged with de facto sovereignty. The First World War became Canada's War of Independence.

National self-sufficiency, however, was limited to the army. Severely neglected in 1914, the navy was the first service to fight. Canadian midshipmen died when German battle cruisers sank a decrepit British squadron off Chile.

HMCS *Rainbow* headed south from Esquimalt to meet the German menace, and might easily have shared the same fate. Two submarines, purchased in Seattle by the British Columbia government, defended the coast, along with a Japanese heavy cruiser whose crew could not land in Victoria because of anti-Asian prejudice. Later in the war, when German U-boats menaced Canada's Atlantic coast, the navy bought trawlers, armed them with old guns, and called them the Halifax Patrol. Their score was zero. It was an embarrassing first round in the Canadian navy's recurrent war on submarines.

Air power helped shape the ground war but, unlike the Australians, Canada left flying to the British. Hundreds, then thousands, of young Canadians joined the British army and navy flying services, which merged in 1918 as the Royal Air Force (RAF). In 1917, Britain even came to Canada to recruit and train flyers. Canadians were free of the working-class accents that offended recruiters looking for "officers and gentlemen." Many of them had experience in a key skill for early air aces: mastering the "deflection angle" or "lead" needed to shoot down birds or airplanes. By war's end, a quarter of the RAF's flyers were Canadians and a Canadian commanded the bomber force preparing to attack Berlin. Ottawa finally authorized two Canadian squadrons—too late for any fighting. Several Canadians became "aces"—Billy Bishop, W. G. Barker and Raymond Collishaw, among others—but few back home realized Canada's important role. The RAF had its own publicity priorities!

Canadian Corps victories in 1918 were a far cry from the murderous futility of the offensives on the Somme in 1916. They owed little to tanks, aircraft and other new weapons, a lot to painfully acquired military competence, and most of all to an abundance of Canadian personnel. This was one result of the passage of the Military Service Act (MSA) in 1917. Americans had conscripted from the outset but had hardly begun to fight when the war ended. By 1918, the British were conscripting men from seventeen to fifty years old. Conscription guaranteed personnel for the Canadian Corps from 1917, and made its last volunteers available for its great battles in 1918, since it could ensure their replacement. Only in October 1918 did "MSA men" begin to join the Corps.

Later, with the sudden victory in 1918, the cost of the MSA seemed to outweigh the benefits. Conscription enraged French-speaking Quebec, whose Canada began in Canada, not in Flanders. French Canadians were not alone.[5] Farmers needed their sons, unions condemned compulsion, radicals and pacifists denounced the war itself. Others quietly hoped to avoid military service. All resented the pro-MSA majority, but Quebec would remember longest.

Except at military museums and memorials, conventional Canadian history now pays little attention to the feats of the Canadian Corps and, in Quebec, almost none. The 1918 victories are ignored, credited to the Americans or dismissed because the Germans were exhausted. Instead, Canadians learn about women as nurses and munition workers, the grievances of

---

5. Depending on the militia to recruit volunteers underlined the weakness of the force in Quebec. As an outspoken Orangeman from Ontario, Sam Hughes was ill-equipped even to recognize the problem, much less solve it. A lone francophone battalion, the 22nd or "Van Doos," served with the Corps from 1915. Another French-speaking unit, held in England, was broken up in 1918 to fill the Van Doos' exhausted ranks.

farmers and industrial labour, and the folly of conscription. War history focuses on the futility of the Somme and the ineptitude of generals. It is, of course, a people's perspective. Even soldiers in the Canadian Corps disliked General Currie—"Guts and Gaiters" was a printable nickname. Most soldiers spent about a year at the front line and few recognized changes in tactics, weapons and competence. Afterwards, wartime propaganda smelled like a pig barn and its practitioners, pre-war literary heroes, faded fast from public taste.

The war cost Canada sixty thousand lives, and as many more were so maimed in mind or body that they could never again live normal lives. Caring for them and twenty-five thousand widows and orphans was a huge new cost for a country that had quintupled its national debt. Few Canadians in 1919 felt victorious. War had been a nightmare. Half a century earlier, Canadians had concluded that, if they didn't want another war, a wise policy was not to prepare for it. The wartime colonels and generals who staffed the post-war defence forces disagreed, but ignoring war made sense to many of their fellow Canadians.

Sir Robert Borden resigned as prime minister in 1920. Apart from a Depression-ridden Tory interlude between 1930 and 1935, William Lyon Mackenzie King led Canada from 1921 to 1948 at the head of a Quebec and prairie coalition. Isolationism was pure political logic, and convenient for a man acutely uncomfortable in the presence of soldiers.[6] Given that

---

6. King shone as a mediator, no bad talent for a Canadian prime minister. He had actively promoted the 1914 peace centennial project and he owed his leadership to running for the Laurier Liberals in 1917. Fortunately for him, his discreet offer to run for Borden's Unionists was unknown or forgotten.

Communists and labour radicals threatened turmoil, King was too conservative to abolish the militia, as pacifists and some in Quebec would have liked, but in 1922 he bundled the army, navy and a new Canadian air force into a single Department of National Defence. His new defence minister promised something "inexpensive but snappy," and then virtually closed down the navy by getting rid of most of its ships. The new air force was practically forced on Canada in the form of a large dowry of RAF post-war cast-offs. It promptly showed the government what aircraft could accomplish on Canada's huge, unpopulated frontier by spotting forest fires and delivering treaty payments to remote Aboriginal bands.

As for the army, it reverted to its pre-war structure. A few CEF battalions became militia regiments but usually languished; the old regiments had clout enough to grab the honours of CEF units, and the social prestige to survive neglect. Militia now wore khaki uniforms as well as costly full dress, but government economy drives allowed even less training than before the war. The Permanent Force expanded slightly to accommodate skeleton versions of two famous CEF units, Quebec's Royal 22e Régiment (the "Van Doos") and Princess Patricia's Canadian Light Infantry (PPCLI) for the West. Veterans filled the officer positions, waiting to regain their wartime ranks. Promotion came with seniority and a spotless record of avoiding controversy. Professional thought seemed irrelevant. Either there would be no war or "mechanization" would change it beyond recognition. If there were useful new ideas, the British would provide them. Officers from all three Canadian services got their only serious military training in England. In the 1920s, as Canada became the world's second largest automotive producer, the militia stuck to horses.

How did official Ottawa remember the war? During 1915–18, a wealthy Canadian expatriate, Max Aitken (Lord Beaverbrook), managed the propaganda extolling the Canadian Corps. He also created an elaborate Canadian War Records Office, with art, film, artifacts and documents, and planned for a great museum in Ottawa, on the scale of the Australian War Memorial in Canberra. After 1918, his plan was buried. Ottawa's memorializing focused on war art and a Peace Tower for the new Parliament buildings, rebuilt after a 1916 fire. Sam Hughes had appointed Ernest Cruikshank, a militia colonel, official historian for the CEF. Cruikshank's story of the Great War began in 1763! Colonel A. F. Duguid, a McGill-trained engineer and artillery veteran, replaced him in 1921, only to be utterly distracted by queries from superiors, disputes over battle honours, and efforts to protect the CEF's reputation from British historians. Duguid's first volume appeared in 1938. A year later, the Great War seemed like ancient history, and an official history was not published until 1962.

In 1930, R. B. Bennett won the federal election, in part because he had opposed conscription in 1917. His government promised military reform—more militia training and an RCAF committed to a fighting role. Bennett purchased a few fighters and some British-made machine-gun carriers. Then the reality of the Depression hit. Cancelling civil flying cost the RCAF five hundred air crew—the "Big Cut." The army chief, Major General A. G. L. McNaughton, suggested abolishing the navy and using the RCAF for coast defence. The new network of naval reserve units fervently lobbied politicians, and the navy survived with some bitter memories. McNaughton next proposed that the army organize relief camps for the single unemployed, creating the single most unpopular Bennett policy of the Depression era.[7]

Mackenzie King returned to power in 1935, just in time to stop Canada's support for League of Nations sanctions against Italy for invading Ethiopia. Japan had conquered Manchuria and Hitler was rearming Germany. If Europe went to war, could Canada stay out? King would try. The United States, still resentful of the Allied propaganda that had drawn it into the Great War and of the unpaid war debts of its allies, seemed utterly isolationist. Canada would follow suit. Contacts between senior British and Canadian officers were sharply curtailed. Instead, Canadian officers visited Washington. In 1937, the government allowed rearmament, but with priority for the air force, navy and coast artillery. Canada would defend its own shores and, if necessary, send pilots. Surely air force losses could never lead to conscription. When the British suggested training aircrew in Canada's peaceful skies, Ottawa refused.

True, when Mackenzie King visited Hitler in 1938, he carefully reminded the Führer of Canada's British alliance. The British, who had written off Canada, were astonished. When the Munich Agreement sacrificed Czechoslovakia to gain

---

7. Both Bennett's relief camps and Franklin D. Roosevelt's Civilian Conservation Corps camps across the United States used unemployed men to work for low pay. Unlike Bennett's, the American camps were popular. Was it because CCC members were young and wore smart green uniforms, while Canadian "reliefers" were of all ages, wore cloth caps and baggy cardigans, and the program's military auspices were scrupulously downplayed by all but hostile propagandists? Or was it because the CCC improved parks and nature trails while Bennett's campers often built barracks, airfields and rifle ranges that, until 1939, few Canadians wanted? Relief campers called themselves the "Royal Twenty-Centers," in honour of their meagre daily wage.

"peace in our time," King rejoiced, but when Hitler seized Prague in early 1939, King sadly prepared Canada for a now-inevitable war. A pledge of no conscription, echoed by the Opposition, helped soften Quebec. In June, a first-ever royal visit, by King George VI and Queen Elizabeth, broke the drab Depression mood and revived old loyalties. However unimaginable a year earlier, a united Canada went to war by the vote of its own Parliament on September 10, 1939.[8]

This time, there was no Sam Hughes to rally the troops and not much booming patriotism. Unemployed men, "breadliners," lined up to join the army. A British delegation had to bargain every detail of a British Commonwealth Air Training Plan (BCATP); its members felt incensed when King expostulated, "This is *your* war." Instinctively, the government agreed to send an infantry division: a purely RCAF contingent seemed inadequate, particularly since Canada had barely one ill-equipped squadron fit to send.

History mattered. Almost everything Ottawa did in 1939 borrowed experience from the earlier war. Between 1916 and 1919, inflation had devastated family incomes; in 1939, a Wartime Prices and Trade Board promised action. Profiteering had been a scandal in the First World War; this time, Crown corporations would manage most wartime business. "Dollar-a-year" men would donate their business connections and expertise. Robert Borden had sacrificed Canadians and even his party for victory; this time, Canadian and Liberal interests came first. Like children, generals, admirals and air marshals

---

8. Or so Parliament thought. The declaration got lost and was only signed by the King months later. Canada's armed forces had moved their pitiful resource to war stations on September 1, the day the British went to war, as they had in 1914. Old habits and prudence had combined.

would be seen but seldom heard in government councils, lest their bias infect the government. In 1940, when Hitler's blitzkrieg overran much of Western Europe and Canada suddenly ranked second only to England among his enemies, King allowed conscription through the National Resources Mobilization Act (NRMA), but only for home defence. The army eventually raised its overseas contingent to five divisions, but only with a solemn pledge that volunteers would suffice to fill their ranks.

Borden had used Canada's war effort to negotiate a role for his utter earnestness in guiding the imperial war effort. King had no such desire. If Canada's economy and post-war interests were to be involved, he wanted a voice, but strategy and tactics were for senior allies only. Any Canadian involvement risked added commitments. Belatedly, King realized that his voters took pride in Canada's fighting role, and he became as eager for recognition as any small ally. Otherwise, British and American leaders could manage the war. When Winston Churchill and Franklin D. Roosevelt met twice during the war in Quebec City, King was on hand for photo opportunities; when serious negotiations began, he politely left.

Canada's military leaders reflected their British training. The RCN's regular officers felt at home with the Royal Navy and schemed to emerge from the war with a fleet of major warships. Convoy escorts were usually relegated to reserve officers, raw crews and ill-equipped corvettes, a combination hopelessly outmatched by German U-boats. An Allied conference in 1943 forced the RCN to admit that more training, not more ships, must be its top priority. In turn, the Allies made long-range patrol planes available and allowed a Canadian, Rear Admiral L. W. Murray, to take command of

Allied operations in the Northeast Atlantic off Nova Scotia and Newfoundland.[9]

Ultimately, the RCAF sent forty-six squadrons and thousands of aircrew to Britain, but so many of its personnel were engaged with the Air Training Plan that, by agreement, the ground crew, airplanes and money were provided by the British. So, of course, was command. Since "Canadianization" cost money, it was resisted in Ottawa as well as in Whitehall. Not until late 1942 was the RCAF's 6th Group formed in England as part of the biggest and costliest air operation of the war, bombing the Third Reich. By the end of the war, a fifth of RAF flying personnel were Canadians and forty percent of Canada's forty-four thousand war dead were RCAF personnel. From the frozen seas off Norway to the Burmese jungle, Canadian flyers contributed to the war effort. Yet the highest ranking Canadian airman in an operational command was the equivalent of a major general. In Canada, the RCAF was the service of choice for most young Canadians, but few Canadians knew how big a role it played in the war.

The army's tradition of serving together gave it profile but little romantic appeal. Drawn from retirement because King knew he opposed conscription, General Andy McNaughton delighted journalists when he claimed that Canada's army was "a dagger pointed at Berlin." So it might have been, but it had lost all the skills of the honoured but forgotten Canadian

---

9. Canadian admirals had noticed the navy's defects but Ottawa is a long way from the sea, and peacetime experience had taught commanders at headquarters not to make trouble for politicians. Quantity seemed more useful to powerful ministers like C. D. Howe than quality. The wartime government could hardly admit that Canadian-made H2S radar sets were largely ineffective in locating German U-boats. Nor would their manufacturers. Whom would you blame? Admirals, industrialists or politicians?

Corps. Its generals and staff had few ideas about mechanized warfare, and the few they had were soon proved wrong by wartime experience. The disastrous Dieppe raid in 1942 showed Canadians how poor their training had been. A year later, when the 1st Division landed in Sicily, few of its original "breadliners" were still with it. It had an easier introduction to battle than its predecessor in 1915 and, in Major General Guy Simonds, a better commander. A Permanent Force artillery captain in 1939, Simonds became the best Canadian field commander since Arthur Currie, though subordinates often found "The Count" cold, arrogant and anglophilic. His superior, General Harry Crerar, once asked the senior army psychiatrist to assess Simonds's mental balance.

Watching Canadians disembark in 1914, a British observer claimed that they would make fine soldiers—if all the officers were shot. Similar comments were made after 1939. By 1943, according to military historian John English, not just McNaughton but most Canadian generals were a problem. Other observers are more charitable. Given that most commanders came from the tiny Permanent Force, average competence was higher than anyone could expect. Ottawa's reluctance to let the army fight reduced both experience and casualties—a trade-off with obvious political benefits. Professional curiosity and intense training, unthinkable in the peacetime army, would have helped. A militia major, Bert Hoffmeister, ended up in a psychiatric ward because he recognized that no one was teaching him what he needed to know to lead troops in battle. A wise doctor sent him back to his unit and Hoffmeister became the best divisional commander in the army. As a young PT instructor, Major General Rod Keller was known as "Captain Blood"; by the time he sent his 3rd Division ashore on D-Day, he was an overweight drunk. British generals questioned his courage. They also criticized Lieutenant General E. L. M. Burns of I Canadian Corps in Italy; subordinates billed him as "Smiling Sunray" for his constant gloom and blamed him for regular "snafus." As the ailing and uncharismatic commander of First Canadian Army, only Crerar's nationality kept him in his job, though no one questioned his courage, political smarts and ability to learn.

By the end of 1944, five Canadian army divisions and a couple of armoured brigades were engaged in Belgium and Holland and northern Italy. Battle-trained generals and colonels had replaced duds. Armour, infantry, artillery and other elements had—at a high cost in lives—learned to work together. Still, front-line morale was in the dumps. While Currie had had enough men in 1918, Crerar did not. Infantry companies had 40 or 50 soldiers to do the work of 150; platoons picked night patrols from 15 men, not 40. Many infantry were plucked from such rear-area jobs as clerks, cooks and mechanics and sent forward with little or no training. If the war had ended late in 1944, as Monday-morning quarterbacks think it should have, there might have been no problem. Instead, fighting continued into 1945.

The generals had promised no conscription. They had not asked to split Canada's army between Italy and France, creating two fat administrative tails. They had not foreseen that home-defence conscripts would cling to their rights until self-righteous patriots called them "zombies." Failing to predict near-annihilation of Hitler's Luftwaffe, the generals had prepared for too many rear-area losses. Remote from the front lines, they might have continued to ignore the problem had Major Conn Smythe, owner of the Toronto Maple Leafs, not gone home and blown the whistle about the lack of men in front-line units, and the burdens that fell on exhausted survivors.

In 1942, King had trumped the Tories by calling a plebiscite on conscription. Most Canadians cheerfully cancelled the promise King had given Quebec in 1939, but still he refused to act. "Not necessarily conscription," he explained, "but conscription if necessary." Was it now "necessary"? J. L. Ralston, his defence minister, went overseas to check. Detailed research told him it was. King called McNaughton from retirement and fired Ralston. McNaughton believed that even "zombies" would heed his call. They didn't. When generals reported the reaction, they were accused of not trying hard enough. When some of them quit, McNaughton called it a generals' mutiny. A frightened King agreed to force fifteen thousand trained infantry overseas. There were riots in Quebec and a brief mutiny at Terrace, near Prince Rupert, but in early 1945, the "NRMA men" went.

And, as in 1918, they weren't needed. Fighting slowed for the winter. While Canada's I Corps in Italy travelled to the Netherlands, only II Corps, in northern Germany's Hochwald Forest, experienced bloody fighting. As in 1918, conscripts joined a victorious army. When war in Europe ended on May 6, 1945, they became part of Canada's promised occupation force. Soon, they came home. Reports of protests and "sit-down strikes" had encouraged Ottawa to cancel a troublesome commitment to share in occupying post-war Germany.

From December 7, 1941, when Japan attacked Pearl Harbor, Canada fought a two-front war. Sending two army battalions to Hong Kong a few weeks earlier to deter a Japanese attack proved doubly futile. Unsurprisingly, Japan did not revise its strategy, and the survivors of a hopeless siege spent forty-two appalling months as prisoners of war. Panic-stricken British Columbians demanded expulsion or captivity for twenty-one thousand Japanese-Canadians. Though navy, army and RCMP officials agreed that internment was unnecessary, British Columbia's cabinet representatives made sure that Ottawa obliged. They also demanded improved defences against a somewhat improbable Japanese invasion. Thousands of home defence conscripts were introduced to the mountains, beaches and persistent dampness of BC. A brigade of NRMA men even joined a bloodless American expedition to recapture Kiska, an island in the Aleutians.[10]

When fighting in Europe ended, the RCN sent major warships to join Britain's Pacific Fleet. The RCAF planned to attack Japanese cities with a twelve-squadron bomber force, and the army organized an infantry division, based on US weapons, organization and tactics. Since Pacific volunteers got priority in the line-up to go home, recruiting was easy. Delivery was not. Fed up with heat and British-style discipline, the crew of a Canadian cruiser off Okinawa complained that they had not voted to serve in the Pacific. Ottawa agreed. A humiliated captain weighed anchor and headed for home. The RCAF learned that Americans had few airfields for

---

10. Had the Kiska expedition in 1912 broken King's pledge to keep NRMA conscripts at home? If they had gone overseas, they would have been exempt from income tax. Revenue was the issue when a Canadian judge decided that Kiska was, in fact, in the western hemisphere.

RCAF bombers. The army's contingent was mostly on leave in August when atomic bombs dropped on Hiroshima and Nagasaki and a Soviet invasion of Manchuria forced out Japan's military junta. On August 14, Emperor Hirohito announced his country's surrender.

4

LAST WAR

THE MORE IDEALISTIC of our ancestors hoped that the 1914–18 war would prove to be "the war to end all wars." A few decades later, my parents' generation referred to the 1939–45 war as "the last war"—but they weren't imagining it would be the final conflict; they were simply marking the biggest event in their adult lives. Both my parents had been children in the earlier war—my mother recalled that on August 4, 1914, as a precociously literate girl, she had processed the huge newspaper headline into words and ran home to ask her mother what they meant. To me, the "last war" brings memories of rationing, scrap drives, blue aerograms from my distant father and, later, when I learned soldiering at Camp Borden, being told by veteran NCOs what a "real" enemy would have done to me in what *they* called the "last war."

The "last war" is different now. The Cold War ended sometime in 1989 or 1990, almost as vaguely as it had begun. Legally, there was no such war. Practically, it began within days of the Japanese surrender in 1945, though there were no declarations, no "Parliament will decide" and no headlines for a four-year-old to decipher. The Cold War actually began in Canada, rather than any of the familiar news centres of the world. On September 6, 1945, Igor Gouzenko, a cypher clerk at the Soviet embassy in Ottawa, walked out of his workplace with evidence of widespread Soviet spy rings that reached as far as the prime minister's office. The prime minister's initial reaction was to save himself trouble and send Igor Gouzenko back to his employers. It was a nuisance that a wartime ally should have behaved so badly. Instead, Gouzenko went into hiding, and his revelations started the Cold War, though many Canadians modestly would prefer to believe that it started elsewhere—perhaps in Prague in February 1948, when Communists dumped the last democratic government in their region.

Gouzenko's revelations did not stop demobilization in the US or Canada. When service chiefs presented elaborate post-war defence programs, both governments chopped them ruthlessly. There were differences from 1914 and 1939. A monopoly of Hiroshima-era nuclear weapons underpinned America's worldwide power. Beyond Canada's vast Arctic region lay a hostile great power that had not demobilized, ostensibly because of Washington's nuclear threat.

It was tactless to say so amid much global misery, but Canada and the United States had done very well out of the war. Americans were unquestionably the richest people in the world and Canadians were easily in second place. In 1941, most Canadians had definably been poor; by 1951, "poor" people had shrunk to just a third of the population. Reformers credited family allowances; unionists, the right to organize; educators pointed to 280,000 veterans studying at taxpayers' expense. Industrialists and farmers served a world that needed everything Canada could produce. The war had expanded Canada's productive capacity, largely by training factory workers in key industrial skills. Competition would revive someday, but not soon.

That was the good news. The bad news was that, thanks to Gouzenko and much other evidence that followed, both Canada and the United States felt threatened. The peace was no peace. Instead, after two world wars, circumstances promised a third. The two twenty-kiloton explosions that annihilated Hiroshima and Nagasaki promised an ultimate Armageddon. Humanity, and certainly civilization, would perish once nuclear spies and Soviet science broke the US nuclear monopoly. Soviet weapon tests in 1949 warned that the US lead was almost gone. So was immunity from long-range bombing. Americans had developed intercontinental bombers; the Soviets would follow. Japan had threatened Alaska; what could the USSR do?

We know now that some of the fear was groundless. The Soviet Union had suffered horrors in its "Great Patriotic War" that could only be exceeded by nuclear war. At least twenty million of its people had died. Its major cities lay in ruins and the countryside had been ravaged. The USSR had borne the lion's share of the effort it took to defeat Hitler, and was exhausted. Still, the war also taught Soviet leaders that external threats could mobilize their people to make impossible sacrifices. It was so easy to find evidence of American threats that propaganda would have been unnecessary, were it not such a habit. Soviet forces stayed mobilized partly because it was cheaper to billet them in occupied Germany or in newly converted "people's republics" than in the USSR. Soviet physicists and engineers struggled to match a nuclear threat that horrified them as much as it did any American. In any war, the less the other side really knew, the better.

The US and the USSR, along with their respective allies, waged what we can now call "the last war," unless we apply that title to assorted local tragedies that have occurred since 1990.

During the 1939–45 war, Canada had literally switched empires. At Ogdensburg, in August 1940, Mackenzie King placed Canada under the protection of its oldest enemy, the United States. No one was consulted, and hardly anyone complained. After 1945, Canada depended on American capital and markets for its prosperity, and on Washington for its security in a dangerous world. In 1907, Canada had adopted British tactics, doctrine and weapons; in 1948, it switched to the Americans. The Pentagon, not the War Office and Admiralty, became the cradle of our strategy, organization and tools of death.

At first, not much happened. Old habits and sympathies were strong. In the late 1940s, little new equipment was purchased or even available. Americans protected their defence industries with a "Buy America" policy. A dollar-short Canada had little to spend. In uniform, Canada's three services looked as British as ever. Still, the direction was clear. The RCAF, the least nationalist of the services, realized that sharing continental air defence would give it a claim to the most sophisticated aircraft and technology anywhere. Shipboard mutinies between 1947 and 1949 warned the RCN that British-accented officers and British-designed ships made for trouble. Canadian sailors expected US Navy standards of comfort—or better. More than its fellow services, the army had a Canadian identity, but generals soon learned that pressure from Washington to expand Canada's defence effort made civilian policy-makers pay attention. The US had leverage the British never dared use. Hearing them, government ministers might wonder where the loyalty of their admirals, generals and air marshals truly lay.

Chauvinism (the word derives from the name of a notorious Napoleonic colonel) had been widespread among soldiers, but the Allied wars helped make military leaders think transnationally. In 1939, King had privately bemoaned the fact that "a country that has all it can do to run itself should feel called upon to save, periodically, a continent that cannot run itself." Once again, divided and devastated by the war, Europe needed help. In Greece, Italy and France, Communists seemed close to seizing power. A bankrupt, hungry Britain could no longer be Western Europe's guardian. President Truman extended American protection to Greece, financed Christian Democrats in Italy and, when Soviet forces blocked land routes to Berlin, provided hundreds of aircraft to feed the city's western zones of occupation. Canada refused to join the Berlin airlift in 1948, but officials found two good reasons to get involved in Europe. First, the 1939–45 war had persuaded them that isolationism was bankrupt and immoral. Second, Canada needed European influence to balance Washington. In April 1949, the United States, Canada, Iceland and nine European countries, from Norway in the north to Italy in the south, met in Paris and created the North Atlantic Treaty Organization (NATO). A Canadian diplomat called it a "providential solution." By 1957, NATO had fifteen member states.

By 1949, Canada's defences resembled those of 1939. The RCN was bigger by a couple of cruisers and a small aircraft carrier, but most of its warships were destroyers. The land-based "ships" of its reserve were open and looking for part-time volunteers. The pre-war militia had finally won the right to be called the Canadian Army, but its historic units, many of them with wartime roles in the Active Force, found their place in a post-war Reserve Army of—at least on paper—six divisions and several armoured brigades. At twenty thousand, the Permanent Force seemed tiny to its architects and allies, but it was enormous by pre-war standards. Its three infantry regiments and an artillery regiment were organized as an air-portable Mobile Strike Force, with soldiers trained to drop by parachute from Canada's skies on any hostile incursion. With a target of twenty-five thousand full-time members, the RCAF was bigger than the other services combined. Reserve or "auxiliary" squadrons provided the bulk of its flying units, but the air force had money for new aircraft and equipment, and a mandate to provide a market for Canada's post-war aircraft industry. One example was A. V. Roe's CF-100, a twin-engine jet fighter with the long range required to reach Canada's north.

In one key respect, the post-war forces had changed. No official admitted it, but part-time volunteers were no longer Canada's first line of defence. National security depended on "forces in being." Instead of professional stagnation, the three services needed effective military education and training. Modelled on Britain's Imperial Defence College, a new National Defence College in Kingston offered senior officers and their counterparts in the civil service and the private sector a strategic view of defence issues. The air force and army developed their own staff colleges. Most of the fifty thousand permanent members of the armed forces served at scores of training bases, schools and stations.

NATO had little immediate impact on Canadian security. Ottawa's 1949 white paper on defence policy proclaimed that the defence of Canada was the government's top priority: international commitments were well down the scale. Ottawa hastened to transfer Second World War equipment to some NATO partners—only to find that US manufacturers were too back-ordered to deliver replacements.

Like other defence policy statements to come, the 1949 white paper was obsolete within months. On June 25, 1950, the Communist regime in North Korea poured armoured columns into the neighbouring US-backed Republic of Korea (ROK). Despite all the help that US forces in nearby Japan could muster, ROK defences gave way. Urged by the United States, the United Nations approved a US-led "police operation" to drive back the invaders. A Soviet boycott of the UN Security Council prevented a Soviet veto; the first major UN "peacemaking operation" could begin.

Earlier, Mackenzie King had forbidden any Canadian involvement in Korea's post-war settlement. However, his internationalist successor, Louis St. Laurent, was prepared to support collective security. So was Parliament. Three Canadian destroyers sailed at once for the Far East, and the RCAF's 426 Squadron joined the American airlift to Tokyo. As ROK and US troops retreated, Ottawa reluctantly agreed to send troops. It might have sent its regular brigade or mobilized some reserves; instead, it recruited a "special force," primarily from war veterans, using regular force units as a cadre. For the first time, Canada's reserves were left out of a military undertaking.

Helped by a modest recession, a ministerial order to cut enlistment standards and old soldiers who had not adapted to "civvy street," by mid-autumn the army had enough volunteers for two brigades, one for service and the other for replacements. By then, US General Douglas MacArthur had landed troops near Seoul and chased the North Koreans to the Chinese border. His rapid advance and threats brought China, Communist since 1949, into the conflict. Faced with the Chinese onslaught, UN forces fled south, abandoned Seoul and, again, recovered. By the spring of 1951, the United Nations held a line close to the thirty-eighth parallel, the official boundary between the South and North. Soon a Canadian brigade, equipped with aging Second World War weapons, entered the land war as part of a British Commonwealth division. An earlier arrival, a second battalion of the PPCLI, won a US unit citation for helping to repel a major Chinese attack. The war continued until 1953, with nightly patrols, steady losses and desultory truce talks. In all, 20,000 Canadians served a year or less in the Korean War, and 312 Canadian soldiers died.

No sooner had the US mobilized most of its available forces for Korea than a horrible thought struck: what if this was a Soviet feint? After sucking its enemies into a remote Asian war, Stalin's armies could sweep through Western Europe. Washington pulled General Dwight Eisenhower, the wartime Allied commander, out of retirement and sent him to Europe. Passing through Ottawa in January 1951, Eisenhower pleaded for immediate help. St. Laurent responded. Canada would rearm on a scale previously unimagined in peacetime: forty squadrons for the RCAF, twelve of them for European air defence; one hundred ships for the RCN to wage a new battle of the Atlantic; an infantry division for the army, with a brigade of ten thousand soldiers stationed in Europe. After a sharp little fight between generals and air marshals, National Defence Headquarters decided that the RCAF squadrons in Europe would serve with the Americans but the soldiers would be stationed with the British army in Germany. Meanwhile, the government armed itself with an Emergency Powers Act, created a powerful Department of Defence Production for its wartime "Minister of Everything," C. D. Howe, and revisited the problems of "civil defence" in event of enemy attack.

As armed forces personnel grew from 47,000 in 1950 to 104,000 in 1953, familiar issues reappeared. Selected reserve units contributed subunits to the brigade for Europe but the army did not repeat the experiment of building on the militia. Recruits became part of an expanded regular army. NATO doctrine forecast a short, violent war. What was not available in the "shop window" on day 1 would have little or no time to get ready. In Europe, NATO members expected well-trained reserves to augment existing units in a matter of hours.[1] Canada had promised NATO three infantry brigades: two waited in Canada, but would they ever cross the Atlantic? Canadian morale (and behaviour) in Europe improved in 1957 when wives and children crossed the Atlantic to join service members, but few wanted to consider the plight of the families if a shooting war suddenly broke out.[2]

---

1. "Reservists" were typically men who had served as conscripts for two years or less, and who could be called back as trained, if slightly rusty, soldiers. Canada's "reserves" had only as much training and equipment as the various services could afford after the needs of "regulars" were met.

2. Complex plans for repatriation to Canada were developed, but they presumed a slow build-up to the crisis and not the surprise attack NATO propagandists warned about.

Post-war prosperity forced the services to compete for technicians. Having long trained pilots, the RCAF now had to train ground-crew specialists too. Canada's NATO air division took shape only at the end of 1953 but the navy needed another ten years to reach its personnel targets. In 1945, all three services had closed down their women's services; in 1953, the RCAF led the way by reviving its Women's Division. As in previous wars, the army's chief problem was finding infantry volunteers, especially in Quebec. In 1952, even the brigade in Korea lacked the equivalent of two companies. The most serious shortage was in its French-speaking Royal 22e Régiment. Better pay, peace in Korea and, near the end of the decade, another recession eased the army's recruiting problems, but the skills shortage could be tackled only by an expensive commitment to skills training. This was a drain on a defence budget that, by the 1960s, was already compared unfavourably to spending by NATO partners.

Korea and NATO were not the only calls on military personnel. In 1948, Canada provided truce observers for two Commonwealth members, India and Pakistan, after their first round of fighting over the region of Kashmir. In 1956, after Israel and Egypt went to war and Britain and France invaded the Suez Canal zone, Lester Pearson, Canada's secretary of state for external affairs, proposed a UN-run peacekeeping force to separate the belligerents. Furious at their British and French allies, the Americans agreed. Busy suppressing an anti-Communist revolt in Hungary, so did the USSR. Pearson's initiative created a precedent for subsequent Canadian peace-keeping commitments—in the Congo in 1960 and in Cyprus in 1964, where an army battalion would be stationed for almost thirty more years. Other peacekeeping commitments were shorter, and many involved just a few officers or an aircraft or two, but all required trained, available personnel, willing to endure miserable and sometimes dangerous conditions.

Ottawa's chief available motivator for volunteers was pay. For a time, the Canadian Forces were the best paid in the world, a memory that survives only in the minds of aged taxpayers and service veterans. Thanks to selective service—the draft, in popular language—US armed services had no lack of personnel, but foreign wars were unpopular with the relatives and friends of current and potential draftees. In 1952, General Dwight Eisenhower ended a twenty-year Democratic grip on the White House by pledging to end the Korean War. Within a year, "Ike" had kept his promise and started to bring troops home. More significant for Canada was Eisenhower's policy of "more bang for the buck"—which translated as more emphasis on nuclear deterrence and less on costly conventional forces. In response, the Soviet Union tested a megaton-rated hydrogen bomb in 1953 and used Red Square parades to show that it could launch such weapons at North America.[3]

While the US and Canada sustained their NATO commitments, attention turned back to continental defence. The era of weekend fighter pilots and a few old anti-aircraft guns at

---

3. A megaton bomb has the explosive power of a million tons of TNT, not to mention huge heat and nuclear radiation. While Soviet secrecy was proverbial, parades on May Day and Revolution Day gave Soviet forces regular opportunities to showcase their newest weapons to Western military attachés and news media. Sometimes the weapons on display were the only specimens in existence.

Sault Ste. Marie was over. Ottawa announced nine new RCAF squadrons, flying the Canadian-made CF-100 Canuck fighter. By 1954, thirty radar stations along the forty-ninth parallel—a "Pinetree Line"—looked northward. A mid-Canada line of scanning devices along the fifty-fifth parallel took shape in 1955; stations of a Distant Early Warning (DEW) Line sprouted across the Arctic. US radar planes and radar-equipped picket ships watched off the ocean flanks. Whenever the design details were settled, A. V. Roe's futuristic CF-105 Arrow would replace the CF-100 "Clunk," already too slow to catch Soviet bombers. The RCAF was ecstatic; Defence Production Minister C. D. Howe was not. To Parliament he confessed, "We have started a program of development that gives me the shudders." Those shudders, inherited by John Diefenbaker's Progressive Conservatives when they defeated the Liberals in 1957, ended the Arrow program in 1959. Americans filled the hole with the F-101 Voodoo, a supersonic fighter relegated to the Air National Guard, and the Bomarc, an anti-aircraft missile that made nonsense of the government's claim that it had scrapped the Arrow because intercontinental ballistic missiles (ICBMs) were now the threat.

The Americans gave lots of help. From 1949, Canada was treated as an extension of the United States for foreign military aid procurement. A defence production sharing agreement followed the Arrow cancellation. US taxpayers paid for the DEW Line and, except for a sector that covered Montreal and Toronto, as well as New York and Philadelphia, the US Air Force and Navy provided air defence coverage for most of the continent. Of course, American interests prevailed. When France abandoned NATO's air defence system for reasons of sovereignty, any pretence that NATO extended to North America dissolved.

Americans never wanted foreign meddling with their own security, but agreed in 1957 to a North American Air Defence Command (NORAD), with an American general in command and a Canadian as deputy. With an election imminent, St. Laurent's Liberals hesitated but, to RCAF delight, Diefenbaker signed soon after becoming the first Tory prime minister since R. B. Bennett. He also approved a series of weapons systems with nuclear features, from air-to-air missiles to "Honest John" rockets for Canada's NATO contingent. A robust Cold Warrior who had promised Ukrainian-Canadian audiences to "roll back the Iron Curtain," Diefenbaker was not inclined to question anything President Eisenhower proposed.

NORAD was designed to intercept Soviet bombers but, just as it "stood up,"[4] the threat shifted to unmanned guided missiles. By launching the Sputnik satellite after a series of well-publicized US missile failures, the USSR demonstrated leadership in rocket science. Humiliated, Americans struggled to catch up. Bombers certainly had advantages: human pilots could be instructed and recalled during their flight. Once launched, deliberately or by accident, missiles were irretrievable. Were safeguards on missile bases adequate to prevent human error or mischief? How would nations cope with split-second decision making in a world with nuclear weapons?[5]

---

4. A piece of military jargon for the moment when an organization is ready to function.

5. A Canadian, Dr R. J. Sutherland of the Defence Research Board, added sophistication to deterrent warfare by defining a "first strike, second strike" doctrine. Second strike, or retaliation, was possible only if enough of a nation's missiles and command structure survived the first strike. Protecting them became a top priority.

If an enemy survived a first nuclear strike with enough power to annihilate the aggressor, would there even be a first strike? The doctrine had consequences. To keep them safe, bombers carrying nuclear warheads spent days overhead, with airborne "tankers" to refuel them. Concrete, impact-proofed silos in remote places housed intercontinental ballistic missiles (ICBMs).

Equally, the population had to be assured of its survival. The army's reserve, renamed the Militia, had been dreaming of winning fresh battle honours in a third world war when the bad news broke. Forget about tanks, guns and rocket launchers. The Militia would focus on "National Survival." Army brass fought the order for a year but the new Diefenbaker government insisted. Local armouries were soon festooned with ladders, ropes and first aid equipment; Militia veterans quit in droves. Weakened by post-war prosperity, ample alternatives for recreation and a changing ethos, the Militia faded fast. Meanwhile, local governments acquired sirens and debated evacuation plans. Pamphlets instructed citizens to build and equip a fallout shelter in the basement to preserve their families from the clouds of deadly radiation that would follow a nuclear strike. War, it became clear, was dangerous. Widespread alarm fuelled peace and anti-nuclear movements. A flood of mail troubled the prime minister.

Liberals had sometimes worried about Washington's leadership. During the worst moments of the Korean War, Ottawa feared that President Truman might allow General MacArthur to use atomic bombs, and rejoiced that Clement Attlee, the British prime minister, exercised a moderating influence. Now, as long as President Eisenhower led the alliance, Diefenbaker was too overawed by the wartime leader to argue. Ike's youthful Democratic successor, John F. Kennedy, was another matter. By 1961, crises abounded. To end an exodus of East Germans to the West, Moscow threatened Allied forces in Berlin. Kennedy threatened right back, until East Germany built a wall across the city and the crisis eased. After Cuba's Fidel Castro overthrew a brutally corrupt regime, American-sponsored schemes tried to overthrow the new regime. They failed, and Castro embraced Communism and turned to Moscow for aid. The Soviets sent ballistic missiles to back up the Castro regime. By October 1962, the Americans felt deeply threatened. For eight days, Washington and Moscow exchanged ultimata, threats and muffled hints of compromise. Meanwhile, most North Americans awaited a thermonuclear holocaust. I recall standing beside an empty truck on a Camp Borden parade square, designated to rescue survivors from the Toronto area. I wondered what possible use we would be.

The Cuban Missile Crisis of 1962 had some specific Canadian consequences, which are described in Chapter 9. For most of the world, the mutually assured destruction of nuclear strategy came closer than ever before or since. Whether or not Nikita Khruschev blinked before Kennedy, both sides made concessions. Soviet missiles left Cuba but US invaders never landed, and American missiles left Turkey. The Cold War entered a stalemate. Annual NATO and NORAD exercises became rituals, altered only by fresh military technology.

Superpower rivalry now played out in newly independent and often impoverished nations of the Third World, where righteous neutrality usually coincided with demands for costly weapons to pursue old enmities. The best known of these wars, inherited from France, was the ideological-ethnic struggle in Indochina that Americans came to know as the Vietnam War. There were many others, from the Indo-Pakistan wars over Kashmir, Arab-Israeli wars in the Middle East, and guerilla wars from Peru to Angola and the Philippines to Afghanistan. All of them devastated the economies and environments of poor countries and dismayed, then exasperated, people in wealthier nations. They also provided sales and testing opportunities for members of what President Eisenhower had called the "military-industrial complex."

How did these wars affect Canada? Imperceptibly. Vietnam, Angola and even Peru seemed far away. Canadians returned to their customary feelings of invulnerability. Basement fallout shelters resumed their former role of storing garden tools and disused toys. The Militia gradually shed its National Survival duties and, after a significant trimming of the number of units and the sell-off of many small-town armouries, was allowed operational training. Many of its cadres had long since quit in disgust. The terrors and temptations of a third world war grew farther away than ever. Militia units, supplanted by the regular army in the 1950s as Canada's first line of defence, now existed mainly to augment their costly rivals in the regular army with their best soldiers.

In 1968, Trudeaumania gave Canada a new Liberal prime minister and virtually a new government. Pierre Elliott Trudeau personally espoused such warrior virtues as courage, fitness and asceticism, but he despised military minds and their "strategists' cramp." Trudeau would have eliminated Canada's NATO commitments; under pressure, he merely cut Canada's forces in Europe by half. "Priority One" on Trudeau's list was defending Canada. Peacekeeping, number one for Lester Pearson, dropped to fourth place, behind NORAD and NATO. Priority One included the creation of a northern headquarters at Yellowknife, increased aerial surveillance in the Arctic—and deploying most of the army on Operation ESSAY, in response to the October Crisis of 1970. Trudeau policies included bilingualism and scores of French Language Units (FLUs) for the Canadian Forces.

The outsized post-war generation, larger in Canada than anywhere else, showed little sympathy for military values or Cold War preoccupations. Their era promoted two main causes, feminism and the environment. One consequence was pressure on the major powers to constrain the nuclear testing programs that had continued through the 1950s. Protests in the 1960s terminated open-air American tests. Greenpeace, founded in Vancouver in 1970, proved to be the most determined of many groups formed to protect the planet from those who prepared for war. In 1972, it mobilized well-publicized protests against French nuclear tests in the Pacific.

Like the protesters, Trudeau and his entourage presented a frontal challenge to much that was familiar and traditional in defence circles, from alliance strategies to the exclusion of women from influential roles. The navy lost its aircraft carrier, despite a costly refit; the army lost historic regiments; the air force waited an extra decade to replace obsolete aircraft. NATO had long provided the three services with ready-made arguments for the modern weapons, equipment and training needed if Canadians were to "fight the best alongside the best." After 1968, NATO arguments only had leverage if they fitted Trudeau's priorities. Eager to replace its obsolete British tanks but aware that armour had no obvious role in Canada's home defence, the army found an ally in German Chancellor Helmut Schmidt. Trudeau's agreement to buy German tanks bought Schmidt's support for Canadian membership in the Group of Seven industrialized countries. Such opportunities were rare—defence ministers seldom won cabinet support for costly programs. By the 1980s, DEW Line equipment was so obsolete that spare parts came from Communist Czechoslovakia. The navy's youngest ship dated from 1971. The army's newest weapon was the Cougar, a wheeled, lightly armoured vehicle, which could withstand rifle bullets and stones. Armoured units used it as a make-believe tank.

Trudeau's tough-minded logic and uncomfortable questions tested Canada's defence establishment, though pro-military critics have written of "a dark night of the soul." Largely absent was a searching review of value obtained for dollars spent. In the 1980s, it was common to complain that Canada's defence spending represented the lowest share of gross national product of any NATO member but tiny Luxembourg and unmilitary Iceland. Given the level of threat to Canada, was that a rational premium? What might have been asked was why Canada, which actually spent more money in absolute terms than most NATO countries, got so little for its dollars. The Dutch, with a similar standard of living and almost identical spending, provided NATO with a modern navy and air force and an army corps of two divisions—at a time when Canada mustered only obsolete ships and aircraft and an under-strength mechanized division with worn-out weapons.

The Dutch, of course, conscripted young men and paid them far less than the salaries Canadians expected for military service, especially when posted to Europe. Canadian equipment purchases had always involved politics, right back to the 1880s decision to dress the militia in high-cost, low-quality Canadian-made uniforms in deference to Sir John A. Macdonald's National Policy. Replacing the US-built fighters of the post-Arrow era led to furious debates about regional benefits. When Ottawa finally chose the McDonnell-Douglas CF-18, a rival American manufacturer intervened during the 1980 Quebec sovereignty referendum to proclaim that the decision was intended to punish Quebec's aircraft industry. Since politics determined the opening and closing of bases, the Department of National Defence was one of the largest landholders in Canada, and one of the most wasteful. Ideally, of course, all defence spending is wasteful since, hopefully, what it buys will never be used. However, the list of beneficiaries could have been smaller.

During Trudeau's regime, the United States had other foreign preoccupations, from Vietnam to Iran. If President Richard Nixon had ended the war in Vietnam, he could have won re-election without resorting to "dirty tricks" like Watergate. His agreement with Soviet leaders to limit anti-ballistic missile (ABM) development was almost the only check he imposed on the Cold War arms race.[6] Critics complained that the US exported the cost of the Vietnam War to its trading partners, but its economy rapidly recovered.

---

6. Canadians have always supported the ABM treaty. It allowed each side to protect a site. The Soviets protected Moscow; the Americans put their missiles around an ICBM site at Grand Forks, North Dakota. Most Canadians rejoiced; only insiders noted that the "killing ground" for incoming missiles would be Manitoba. Fortunately for Canada, the US eventually abandoned even this site.

The Canadian dollar, close to par or at a premium over the American dollar in the early 1970s, soon slumped. In the face of an Arab-dominated petroleum cartel, both economies struggled with energy prices. Meanwhile, the Soviet Union developed and targeted a fleet of intermediate-range nuclear missiles (SS-20s) on NATO capitals.[7] Peace activists ignored the Soviet initiative—until NATO proposed to counter with missiles of its own. A new Ballistic Missiles Early Warning System (BMEWS), with stations in Alaska, Greenland and England, allowed Washington to compensate for DEW Line deficiencies. When Jimmy Carter, a deeply devout peanut farmer, was elected as US president in 1976, Trudeau found an ally in seeking détente. Ronald Reagan's victory four years later brought a strongly conservative edge to United States politics, but it was his defence program that strained Ottawa–Washington relations. An unabashed Cold Warrior, Reagan determined to revive the struggle with what he called "the Evil Empire." Voters wanted him to restore American global power after Carter-era humiliations by Islamic revolutionaries in Iran. A renewed arms race was fed by visions of huge Soviet tank armies menacing Europe, missile-launching submarines in the Arctic, and Soviet fleets challenging US naval dominance in distant oceans.

Reagan's goals included nuclear parity in Europe and the hugely expensive Strategic Defence Initiative, designed to destroy Soviet missiles before they landed. ABM technology resembled shooting a bullet to hit a bullet, and many doubted

---

7. SS means surface-to-surface, like Hitler's Second World War V-bombers. An SAM is a surface-to-air missile, and an ABM is an anti-ballistic missile, designed for the inconceivably difficult task of intercepting a missile in flight.

that it could be done. Reagan was no doubter. Peace move-ments, quiescent for a decade, re-emerged in the eighties, with reinforcements from a much younger environmental move-ment. While Trudeau annoyed peace activists by allowing Americans to test subsonic cruise missiles in the Subarctic, he shared their concern that a nuclear war was dangerously close. Trudeau lectured NATO on its old-fashioned views and signalled his 1984 retirement by touring world capitals to promote peace.

By then Canadians were fed up with the Liberals, and in 1984 John Turner, Trudeau's successor, lost badly to Brian Mulroney's Progressive Conservatives. Mulroney had different priorities. "Good relations, super relations with the United States will be the cornerstone of our foreign policy," he told the *New York Times*. The new government pledged to repair Trudeau-era neglect of the armed forces, despatched fifteen hundred reinforcements to enlarge Canada's NATO brigade in Europe, announced distinct uniforms for the navy, army and air force, and ordered a Swiss-designed anti-aircraft system—to be built in a cabinet minister's Quebec constituency. Plans for an electronics factory in Prince Edward Island faded after voters there elected a Liberal provincial government while an order for six new patrol frigates, built in the Saint John dockyard, was doubled after New Brunswick's Liberal government endorsed Mulroney's constitutional reforms.

The Conservatives had promised a thorough review of Canada's defences. With the government getting through three defence ministers in quick succession, it took several years. In 1985, the United States sent an icebreaker through the Northwest Passage to assert its view of freedom of the seas and its territorial claims. In 1986, an elaborate military exercise demonstrated what many suspected: Canada's longstanding pledge to deliver a brigade group to NATO's Norwegian flank proved unworkable. The commitment was quickly buried.

In 1987, the latest Tory defence minister, Perrin Beatty, released a white paper, *Challenge and Commitment*. An elegant example of "communications strategy," it mixed words of peace and peacekeeping with Cold War graphics. Beatty pledged to double Canada's NATO commitment to two mechanized divisions, backed by forty thousand militia. A third division and a rebuilt North Warning System would protect Canada. So would additional patrol aircraft, new anti-submarine helicopters and a dozen nuclear-powered submarines capable of operating in all three of Canada's oceans. Not since NATO's early years had a Canadian government sounded more belligerent.

For a few weeks, some Canadians actually debated defence. The proposal for nuclear-powered submarines soon sank. Environmentalists denounced the power source, nationalists insisted that the Arctic should be demilitarized and business was shocked at an eight billion–dollar price tag. But it was the Americans who killed the proposal. Having no wish to share nuclear technology or Arctic waters with Canadian warships, the Pentagon warned off French and British suppliers. Canadians would not patrol the polar ice cap any time soon. A new defence minister soon replaced Beatty and applied an alternative government policy: deficit reduction and budget cuts. The peace movement rejoiced but gave the Tories no credit.

Like earlier white papers, *Challenge and Commitment* was simply wrong: by 1988, it was evident that the Soviets were not coming. Even in 1987, the Soviet economy displayed symptoms of strangulation. Matching Reagan in the arms race proved impossible for them. Could massive restructuring—*perestroika*—inspired by enlightenment—*glasnost*—offer a cure?

Mikhail Gorbachev had reached the Kremlin in 1985, before Beatty's white paper reached its first draft, and promptly ended the Soviet war in Afghanistan. Like their American counterparts after Vietnam, Soviet soldiers came home bitterly disillusioned. Like the Americans, their war machine had failed at the hands of tough, untutored guerillas with hand-held weapons. In the 1970s, Nixon's off-loading of Vietnam war costs gave Americans prosperity. In the 1980s, Gorbachev's political and economic reforms shook a corrupt Soviet system to pieces. Across Eastern Europe, dissidents moved from prison to power. On November 9, 1989, East Germany announced that its border with the West was open. Crowds surged to the Berlin Wall, daubed it with slogans and then demolished it.

The Cold War never actually began or ended—but suddenly it had become the "last war."

5

POST-WAR

THE QUIET, unpredicted meltdown of the Soviet Union revealed both the limitations of political prophecy and the power of ethnic nationalism. For all the billions lavished on providing accurate intelligence to governments, corporations and the media, virtually no one predicted the Soviet collapse. And few expected that the emotions Communists had tried hardest to suppress would prove more powerful than Marxism-Leninism. As former Soviet republics broke away from the new Russia, ethnic conflict broke out in most of them. By 1991, it had virtually dissolved the USSR and spread to Yugoslavia.

Far from enjoying the end of the Cold War, much of the world saw an opportunity to settle old scores. When Iraq's military dictator, Saddam Hussein al Takriti, attacked Iran, the United States approved. After Saddam's ten-year war fizzled in 1990, he seized Kuwait. US President George Bush, Ronald Reagan's successor, responded indignantly both to the open aggression and to the threat to Persian Gulf oil supplies.

The US, Britain, France and Italy, liberated from any threat from the East, shipped their NATO heavy weapons to the Gulf and prepared for war.

President Bush expected Canada's prompt support and Brian Mulroney felt strong pressure to provide it. Most Canadians, however, were surprisingly cool to the Gulf crisis, and majority support for President Bush's war came only after fighting broke out. Still awaiting its first new warships since 1973, the Royal Canadian Navy refurbished an old destroyer and frigate and a supply ship, and despatched them. A CF-18 squadron, formed from Canada's NATO contingent, followed. So might have Canada's NATO brigade, but the cabinet agreed that the cost of equipment, reinforcements and transportation was simply too high. So, too, was the risk of casualties. When the Gulf War finally began in January 1991, Americans unleashed sophisticated electronic warfare and tonnes of old-fashioned explosives; Iraqi defences collapsed, and Kuwait was liberated amid the stench of burning oil wells. Saddam's regime survived, largely because Bush and the Pentagon could think of no one who could replace him. While other allies boasted of their role in an easy victory, Canadians rejoiced that all the 2,400 men and women who served in the country's fifth war of the century came home safely.[1]

Peacekeeping was not quite so bloodless. Canadians—and their leaders—believed that kindly soldiers in UN-blue berets contributed to Canada's splendid worldwide reputation; the more peacekeepers the better. Yet before 1990 and often after, peacekeepers appeared when there was no peace to keep and

---

1. Some would report a "Gulf War syndrome," variously attributed to combat stress, chemical weapons or the side effects of depleted uranium.

when their presence served one side. This was particularly true of the breakup of Yugoslavia after 1991. In Sarajevo in 1992, Yugoslav troops under Canadian protection were killed by Bosnian Muslims; near Medak in 1993, Canadian troops fought Croat forces bent on slaughtering Serbs; at Srebrenica in 1995, UN troops from the Netherlands looked on help-lessly as Serb troops massacred Muslims. In 1999, Belgrade was bombed in a largely fruitless attempt to save Albanian-speaking Kosovars. Canadian peacekeepers suffered death and wounds, but it always seemed impolitic for Ottawa to publicize the cost. By killing Belgian paratroopers, Rwanda's Hutu majority scared governments into withdrawing their contribu-tions to Major General Roméo Dallaire's UN peacekeeping force. Then they slaughtered their Tutsi former oppressors. Only Ghanaian troops stuck by the Canadian general: UN officials and the great powers looked elsewhere.

One reason was the Somalia experience. In 1992, Americans invaded the starving country after media reports showed that UN forces had failed to protect food aid workers from local armed gangs. To support the US and give profile to the army, Canada sent its little-used Airborne regiment, knowing it was fit to fight, if not ideal for peacekeeping. At Belet Huen, the Canadians found anarchy and thievery, not war. Hostility with the locals culminated on March 16, 1993, when some soldiers beat a young infiltrator to death. A soldier recorded the crime on videotape. In Ottawa, civil and military officials did what they could to "control" the event. Their new minister, Kim Campbell, seemed destined to be Mulroney's successor and did not need trouble. The videotapes foiled them. Images of peacekeeping would henceforth include the bound, beaten body of Shidane Arone.

The Somalia affair occurred as the Tory government headed for the worst defeat in Canada's political history. In 1992, Mulroney had disbanded Canadian forces in Europe; his successor, Kim Campbell, cancelled part of an order for EH-104 helicopters needed to replace aircraft bought in the Diefenbaker years. None of it cut into their forty billion–dollar deficit or a brutal recession that voters linked, perhaps unfairly, to the new goods and services tax and a hurried free trade deal with the United States.

On October 25, 1993, Jean Chrétien led the Liberals back to power. He had opposed most Tory policies, from free trade to the Gulf War and improved defences. Chrétien kept his promise to cancel the rest of the helicopters,[2] fired the admiral who had been Chief of Defence Staff when Shidane Arone died, and promised a searching investigation.

Initially, Somalia was not the Canadian Forces' biggest worry. Had Liberals acquired new ideas in opposition? Led by University of Toronto professor Janice Stein and Trudeau's former chief of staff Tom Axworthy, a Toronto-based Council of 21 had proposed a "no-war" defence policy. Scrap the navy and air force, it urged, adapt the army for peacekeeping, and save billions. Who needed warriors? Enlisting youngsters for a few years' service would alleviate youth unemployment. Retired Admiral Chuck Thomas had a different vision. Since

---

2. Eight years and a heavy penalty later, his government had to buy other helicopters. Though costly, the EH-104 met Canada's two distinct needs, search and rescue and anti-submarine patrols, with a single model and a single set of manuals and spare parts. Inflation and the reduced post–Cold War market made new equipment expensive. When search-and-rescue helicopters were eventually purchased in 1999, they were EH-104s with a new name ("Cormorants"), reduced capability and a higher price tag.

the navy and air force had new equipment and army equipment was obsolete and costly, Canada should get rid of soldiers and specialize in ships and planes.

Beyond budget-balancing, Chrétien actually had no agenda. His major defence policy statement, released in September 1994, announced that Canada's forces would still be designed to fight "alongside the best, against the best." The cuts came later: personnel would shrink by a quarter, to sixty thousand regulars and twenty-three thousand civilians. Two of three service colleges closed. So did the National Defence College, too notorious for its world tours and conventional thinking. A score of Canadian Forces bases, several of them on expensive urban land, were sold. The defence budget, twelve billion dollars under Mulroney, shrank rapidly to eight billion. Most Canadians, preoccupied by job losses and fading resources for medicare, failed to note the defence cuts; even fewer cared.

The media fixated on Somalia and the promised judicial inquiry. Probing soon switched from the crime at Belet Huen to the failure of colonels and generals to foresee the tragedy. Why had only the low-ranking soldiers who committed the crime suffered penalties? Why had all sorts of problems, real and imaginary, been concealed? In 1997, a new minister, Douglas Young, fired the Chief of Defence Staff. The government demanded that the Somalia inquiry quit probing and report. Voters that spring re-elected the Liberals. Chrétien then accepted a report that proposed that the Canadian Forces be placed in an ethical and judicial trusteeship. The new defence chief, General Maurice Baril, promised to promote ethics, recruit visible minorities and persuade enough women to join the combat arms to form a fifth of

Canada's soldiers, sailors and aircrew. A new ombudsperson and external review committees joined the defence hierarchy. When media reported harassment and assaults on female members of the Canadian Forces, the Military Police was reorganized under a female Provost Marshal who pledged "zero tolerance" for such offences.

In 2000, Canada joined its sixth war since the beginning of the twentieth century, NATO's intervention in Kosovo. By careful management, Canada formed a small squadron of CF-18s, which were barely "interoperable" enough with US Air Force aircraft to share in even "smarter" bombing raids than those over Baghdad in 1991. When NATO land forces finally invaded in June, a troop of Canadian-built "Coyotes" provided radar surveillance for a British armoured regiment.[3] Later that year, a company of the R22eR landed in East Timor, rebuilt a devastated community, and protected it from Indonesian militia. As part of a new policy of "early in and early out," a small battalion of Canadian peacekeepers went to Eritrea in 2000 to monitor a formal truce—and came home again before they got bored.

In the new century, Canada still wants to do a little good in the world, and to offer its allies a little support. Henceforth,

---

3. As Serb forces ignored the bombing and wandered Kosovo at will, critics cried for land invasion. Humanitarians complained that it was unfair that casualties on both sides were mostly civilian, while fighter-bomber pilots were almost immune to danger. One problem was that the US's seventy-tonne Abrams tanks and thirty-tonne Bradley fighting vehicles could not get across Albania's wintry mountain roads to Kosovo. Canada's twenty-tonne Coyotes had little armour but, when spring sunlight dried the roads, they could travel better than tanks. In battle, the crews hoisted radar masts, checked out trouble and tried to stay out of danger. The Coyote was a classic "niche market" development.

defence policy makers insist, Canadians will go in and come out early, as they did in Eritrea in 2001, before most Canadians had even noticed. Others—perhaps mercenaries from developing countries—must do the long and dangerous peacekeeping jobs.

(Does ancient history have lessons? Once the ancient Romans got tired of the inconvenience, danger and unpopularity of fighting barbarians out on the frontier of their empire, they hired foreign "auxiliaries" to do the fighting for them. Eventually, greedy commanders led the auxiliaries back to Rome and frontier warriors discovered that it was easier and more enriching to beat up on Romans than on the nasty barbarians out on the frontier. Then the Romans hired barbarians to keep the peace—until they, too, came south to see where all the money came from.)

Barbarians and "bandits" may well have been on the minds of the officers and technicians who were changing shifts at "The Mountain" above Colorado Springs on the morning of September 11, 2001.[4] The duty roster put a Canadian navy captain in charge of North American air defence.[5]

Since "I'm sorry" is supposed to be the stereotypical Canadian response whenever anything goes wrong, Canadian

---

4. "Bandit" is air force slang for a hostile airplane. To replace the vanished Soviet threat, NORAD focused on the danger of "rogue" states such as Kim Jong Il's desperately impoverished dictatorship of North Korea.

5. Ever since the Trudeau government scrapped Canada's sole aircraft carrier, commands for genuine four-ring naval captains have been scarce. Nor would the air force give up one of its best jobs, deputy commander at NORAD. However, Canadian exchange officers fill a number of responsible jobs in American headquarters—just as US officers fill some key jobs here.

apologies for what happened that morning to New York's World Trade Center and the Pentagon in Washington should have begun about noon. Instead, Canadian editors and critics spent more energy wondering when and how their prime minister found out about the deadly terrorist attack on two famous American buildings than about Canada's role at NORAD headquarters.

What happened that morning at The Mountain was Standard Operating Procedure (SOP). Planes flying from Boston or other US domestic airports were none of NORAD's business. Simply put, NORAD on September 11 oversaw continent-wide air defence against attacks from *outside* North American airspace. Like the spooks at the famous Central Intelligence Agency (CIA), NORAD had no domestic responsibilities. Elaborate protocols for informing Ottawa about enemy attacks on North America were not relevant either. Watching a Korean airliner approach Alaska was NORAD's duty. Watching bad guys hijack a plane out of Boston was not. Disciplined airmen (and sailors) follow orders.

How did Canada get involved in defending the entire North American continent? Will this responsibility grow? We'll address these questions—but first, let's settle a few more urgent details.

In minutes, a policy that had made sense for almost half a century was changed. Within an hour, NORAD had improvised systems that allowed it to empty the North American skies of civilian air traffic. When flights resumed, both American and Canadian fighters had been redeployed to watch over major cities. US reserve fighter squadrons, providing the bulk of manned interceptors, were activated. Pilots received fresh orders to shoot down any errant domestic airliner as resolutely as they would have destroyed a Russian Tupolev Bear or Bison nuclear bomber.

Much was new after September 11; but even more, history was repeating itself. War in the twentieth century had occasionally come closer to North America than the Japanese aircraft carrier fleet off Hawaii in 1941. In the Second World War, German submarines sank tankers off Miami and ships in the Gulf of St. Lawrence. One German submarine landed a spy in the Gaspé and another placed a robot weather station in Labrador. A Japanese sub lobbed shells at the Estevan Point lighthouse near Vancouver, and paper balloons floated across the Pacific in a failed attempt to start forest fires on the West Coast. In 1917, German diplomats plotted to persuade Mexico to attack the US. Nonetheless, it adds up to pretty small potatoes during a century that saw fifty million human beings slaughtered in various forms of warfare.

Still, Americans and Canadians had sometimes felt endangered before September 11, 2001, and never more so than in August 1940, after French and British armies had collapsed before the German blitzkrieg. All of Western Europe, save Fascist Spain and Portugal, trembled under Hitler's rule. Only a fat old politician named Winston Churchill pretended that he could save Britain and the world's most powerful fleet from the people he called "nazzies." Suddenly promoted to leader of Britain's number one ally, William Lyon Mackenzie King didn't welcome the status. Neither did US President Roosevelt. An early result, as we saw, was the Ogdensburg Agreement, a treaty-by–press release promising the permanent pooling of resources and authority for the joint defence of North America.

Britain, of course, did not fall. Having failed to find American aircraft carriers, the Japanese fleet retreated from Pearl Harbor. Americans, not Germans, invaded Canada, to build the Alaska Highway through Alberta and the Yukon and an oil pipeline from Norman Wells to Whitehorse. Then they built the Crimson Route, a chain of airfields that allowed American warplanes to fly from Montreal to Scotland and the European war. The Permanent Joint Board of Defence, co-chaired by New York's gregarious Mayor Fiorello LaGuardia and a dour Canadian public servant, Colonel O. M. Biggar, dutifully met but discussed little. Americans did what they felt they had to, while Canadians fretted quietly about sovereignty and let it happen. At war's end, Canada bought the US engineering projects, a virtually impassable Alaska Highway and some remote airstrips and hangars, to extinguish any conceivable US claims. Ottawa rejoiced when Americans agreed to share costs for the Arctic warfare research centre at Churchill, Manitoba. When Canada attracted Newfoundland into Confederation, it recognized that local US naval and air bases were a key prop under the Rock's economy.

Canadians were anxious about their neighbour, but they had long since evolved from nervous defiance to nervous acceptance. Ideally, in a peaceful world, Ogdensburg would have been forgotten with the passage of time, but the post-war world brought threats to North America even greater than those the Third Reich had posed in 1940. Between the United States and the Soviet Union stretched the mass of land and water called Canada, rather like Poland between Russia and Prussia. To keep from being an invasion route, post-war Canada purchased primitive jet fighters from Britain, trained and equipped its tiny regular army as paratroopers to attack Soviet incursions, and searched for Communist spies in its bureaucracy. And Canada sought friends.

In 1931, Canada had been a founding member of the newly named British Commonwealth. Louis St. Laurent, its post-war prime minister, worked hard to extend the Commonwealth to India, Pakistan, Ceylon and other former colonies.[6] Britain's monarch remained Canada's sovereign. However, as Winston Churchill had recognized in 1940, Canada had switched empires. At imperial conferences in 1907 and 1909, Canada and other dominions had agreed to model their armed forces on Britain's, a choice that made dominion contingents interoperable with British forces in two world wars. Common organization, communications, tactics and training allowed British, Australian, Canadian and South African forces to work together in battle, while adopting the same arms and equipment benefited British manufacturers.

After 1941, Canadian soldiers in the 2nd Special Service Battalion served in an American regiment. Canadians sent to the Aleutians in 1942 adopted American weapons, equipment and even badges. The army's 6th Division, intended for the invasion of Japan, moved to the US in 1945 to be trained and equipped as an American formation.

In February 1947, the Permanent Joint Board's thirty-fifth recommendation committed Canada and the United States to "Adoption, as far as practicable, of common designs and standards in arms, equipment, organization, methods of training

---

6. The word "British" faded discreetly from the title, as "Dominion," at St. Laurent's request, vanished from designations of Canada, partly because it was almost untranslatable into French (*puissance?*) and partly because Sir Leonard Tilley's "dominion under God" had inevitably come to be interpreted as "dominion under Britain."

and new developments to be encouraged, due recognition being given to each country to the special circumstances prevailing therein." At Mackenzie King's insistence, the Board added five clarifying principles, including: "As an underlying principle all co-operative arrangements will be without impairment of the control of either country over activities in its territory."[7]

Service chiefs generally rejoiced. British equipment had often been inferior and certainly scarce. American productivity was legendary and it was just across the border. Navy and air force commanders, more sensitive than their army colleagues to technological innovation, believed that the United States would be the world leader in ships and aircraft.

"Interoperability" with American armed forces—a word not yet invented in 1947—replaced the British interoperability of the previous forty years. In the subsequent half-century, Canadians designed and built their own warships and purchased German tanks, Belgian-designed rifles, British training planes and much else. More and more, though, they bought American, often in complex deals that gave Canadian industries access to US military contracts.

American defence contractors were never cheap. Having made a purchase, Canada sometimes failed to keep up with costly upgrades. In 1981, Canada finally purchased a US navy fighter, the McDonnell-Douglas F-18-A/B Hornet. Ten years later, the Americans had advanced to C/D and E/F models of the F-18, specially equipped to communicate with the US Navy's anti-aircraft cruisers. The US helped Canada adapt its Gulf War squadron in 1991, and it helped again in

---

7. Government of Canada, *Canada Treaty Series*, no. 43 (1947).

1999.[8] Operations went ahead despite Canadian deficiencies and thereby, an American critic complained, increased combat risks for US pilots.

Interoperability is as expensive as keeping up with any neighbour who just happens to be a multi-billionaire. In the Cold War, trying to match American military strength ultimately bankrupted the Soviet Union. Sometimes, Britain, France and, occasionally, other NATO allies surpassed the Americans in a few specialized fields. The alleged superiority of Canada's CF-105 or Avro Arrow to all other fighter-interceptors has become a Canadian national legend. However, on the whole, the Americans produced costly but high-performance arms and equipment and, provided Ottawa could pay, its forces could buy the best available. Like its other NATO allies, Canadians found this a very costly challenge. The price of not buying was and is to look like a poor relation.

Did this make Canada an American colony? Frankly, this is a figure of speech popular chiefly among Canadian nationalists. Washington saw its northern neighbour as both a sovereign country with prickly sensitivity and a partner in vital responsibilities for mutual security. Like other people, most Americans believe that their policies are transcendentally sound, fair and acceptable. They resent the perversity of those who disagree, as Canada did, on issues as sensitive as Castro's Cuban regime, the Vietnam War and the International Criminal Court.

---

8. Canadian pilots lacked night-vision goggles and helmet-mounted bombsight systems, and only some had Nite Hawk Forward Looking Infrared pods. Like other allies, Canadian planes lacked the secure voice communications, "friend-or-foe" identification and data-link interfaces all needed for full interoperability.

After 1940, the United States accepted the lion's share of the cost of defending North America, partly because it wanted the job done well and partly because it recognized that the US, not Canada or Mexico, was the chief target of any aggressor. Still, if Canada really was sovereign, surely it should accept a fair share of the common defence burden. Nothing was more colonial than leaving almost the whole responsibility to the United States, while claiming that neglecting defence implied a superior morality.

Some Canadians insisted that, since American policies make enemies in the world, the United States made itself the major continental target. Would Stalin really have ordered a Soviet H-bomb attack on Canada? Yet most Canadians opposed Josef Stalin's dreams of Communist domination. Should we have allowed North Korea to overrun the South, or the Soviet Union to spread its dictatorship to the English Channel? Should Canadians have disowned the vigorous diplomacy that helped bring the United States into the United Nations or accepted neutrality in the Cold War? Would Canada have settled comfortably with Yugoslavia and Indonesia among the non-aligned nations? In Chapter 6, we shall meet Canadians who have felt this way and who still have influence.

Sometimes, when students complain about Canada's location between the North Pole and the United States, I suggest that they roll up the country like a rug and find it another place on the globe. This is no simple task, given a land mass of 9.97 million square kilometres, none of which they want to leave behind. Usually, they head for the southern hemisphere, often hoping that Australia and New Zealand—or India, South Africa or Argentina—might welcome a new neighbour.

The first discovery is that Canada's climate is not greatly improved by a change of poles, unless you enjoy spending Christmas at the beach and your summer holiday snowboarding. Another, more surprising, revelation is that most alternative neighbourhoods are poorer and a lot more violent. Just like Australia, Canada's huge, empty bulk looks altogether too enticing to rough-looking neighbours. And where is the big, powerful, even reassuring bulk of the United States? Didn't we perform this exercise to leave it behind? Yeah, but . . .

So back we go, conscious that the constraints on a small country with a superpower neighbour are real but that so are some benefits. Geography and history have so far been generous to Canada, and her political managers have only occasionally been fools.

6

PEACE MOVEMENTS

IF CANADA HAS BEEN, for most of its existence, indefensible, undefended and free from attack, why not make this state a matter
of pride and principle? Why not think of our nation, which is
sometimes considered short of identity and patriotism, as a
beacon to the world? Why leave the national distinction of
having no armed forces to Iceland and Costa Rica?

In every generation, some Canadians have urged peace as a
defining characteristic of their country. Some have promoted
Canada as a natural arbitrator and mediator amid the world's
conflicts. A few have made a personal commitment to pacifism, for religious or moral reasons, at whatever cost. For most
Canadians, war and social violence are morally or spiritually
evil, and for a few, they represent crimes they must not
commit under any imaginable circumstances. As we shall see,
more people considered killing to be an intolerable evil until
a worse evil appeared. Such, for a reluctant majority of
Canada's peace movement, was German militarism in 1914
and Adolf Hitler's Nazism in 1939. The advent of nuclear

weapons of mass destruction in 1945, and the recognition of their deadly side-effects, gave the anti-war debate a new, more pervasive significance.

Though the evidence is imperfect, Canadians are often told that we are peaceable by nature as well as by circumstance. Our domestic history has been non-violent to the point of boredom. Canadians do not execute criminals and so feel a little superior to our neighbours, who do. After each world war, Canadians boasted that they had gained nothing of material benefit, beyond the right to a greater voice in the world's affairs. Since Canada helped broker peacekeeping in 1956, preserving peace in trouble spots became the only widely accepted role for Canada's armed forces, and justification for the only major military monument in Ottawa since 1939.

Peacemaking has a long history in Canada. Iroquois lore recalls that the great peacemaker, Dekanahwideh, crossed Lake Ontario in a miraculous stone canoe to bring peace to five warring nations and unite them in a single Confederacy. In Europe, pacifism reached its strongest form among the Quakers and two breakaway sects of German Anabaptists, the Mennonites and Hutterites. Many Quakers and Mennonites settled in the Thirteen Colonies, welcomed British laws exempting them from militia service, and followed the Loyalists northward to find similar guarantees in Upper and Lower Canada. In return, the British authorities (and Canada) gained law-abiding and hard-working settlers.

Religious pacifism has a continuous history in Canada since the 1780s. By the 1820s, legislatures had eliminated fines in lieu of military service. The 1868 Militia Act exempted Quakers, Tunkers and Mennonites from military service, along with judges, convicts and the feeble-minded. When

Canada invited Hutterites, Doukhobors and other pacifist sects to bring their farming skills to the "Last, Best West," exemption from military service was cheerfully conceded. The 1917 Military Service Act bypassed the Militia Act, but the earlier pledge was resentfully if selectively respected. Groups explicitly exempted from service in the Militia Act or in immigration agreements qualified for exemption; other sects did not.

Secular pacifism grew out of political ideas. Henry Wentworth Monk, son of a British half-pay officer who settled near Ottawa, grew up as a devout Anglican, but embraced millenarian Zionism. Only when Jews returned to the Holy Land, Monk believed, could Christ's Second Coming occur. Monk twice went to Palestine and came to believe that only a world council, located in Jerusalem, could save civilization from world wars. British backers paid him to go to Washington and end the US Civil War. He failed. After surviving an 1864 shipwreck on the coast of Maine, Monk's mind and health were damaged, and he lived near Ottawa until 1896 as Canada's best-known pacifist and Zionist.

Utopian thinkers like Monk were more common in the United States than in Canada; in the US, early adoption of radical technological changes—railways, steamers, telegraphs—invited radical ideas. Such inventions in communications, Monk argued, made world government practical. Europeans were tradition-bound but young countries could innovate. And who could deny, after six hundred thousand people died in the American Civil War, that war was an evil? People united by religious faith and a belief in human perfectibility could agree that the abolition of war required no more than a strenuous will to do right. By the end of the nineteenth century, many farm organizations, Protestant congregations, labour unions and women's groups had endorsed peace and denounced militarism.

Women provided an obvious force for peace—the nineteenth century proclaimed women's moral superiority. What responsible mother could raise her boy to be a soldier unless it was to fight an immoral enemy, like the slave-holding Confederates of the American South? In 1874, Letitia Yeomans launched the Women's Christian Temperance Union: peace and Prohibition became logical partners for women battling male self-indulgence and violence. In 1893, Lady Aberdeen, wife of the Governor General, summoned Canada's most prominent women to Ottawa and created the National Council of the Women of Canada. At Dundas, near Hamilton, Adelaide Hoodless, whose young son had died from impure milk, launched the first Women's Institutes to campaign for pasteurization, public health and, soon, for peace. By 1912, one Canadian woman in eight belonged to an organization, and most of them stood for peace.

So did farmers. Not only were they the most righteous of producers, but they also had a deep aversion to taxes. What benefits did they gain from defence spending? Labour had a more practical concern: in the new century, troops were often summoned to break strikes. Not only then should working men refrain from joining the militia, but they must also abstain from capitalist wars. In 1912, Canada's Trades and Labour Congress approved uncompromising opposition to war. So had Methodists, Congregationalists and clergy in many other Protestant denominations. Was not Christ the Prince of Peace? What part of the commandment "Thou shalt not kill" was unclear?

The South African crisis of 1899 challenged Canada's peace advocates. It split the federal cabinet and sent Canadians into the Boer War more divided, according to historian C. P. Stacey, than in any later war. French Canadian objections to fighting in imperial wars were well known; influential English-speaking Canadians like Richard Scott, leader of the Irish Catholics, editors like Joe Atkinson of the *Toronto Star* and respected opinion makers like Goldwyn Smith felt just as strongly. Trapped between imperial and peace sentiments in his own Liberal Party, Laurier temporized for a month. Once committed, however, support for Canada's soldiers in South Africa grew substantially. Women clamoured for war work, money flowed to a Patriotic Fund and Protestant congregations dismissed peace-minded clergy. It was a portent of future imperial struggles.

After the Boers surrendered in 1902, peace revived as a cause. So did militarism, in the form of cadet training in the schools, a spread of rifle clubs and a campaign for universal military training. Yet despite the efforts of prominent businessmen, professors and Edith Boulton Nordheimer of the Imperial Order of the Daughters of the Empire (IODE), militarism made little headway. So many Canadians applauded Laurier's familiar message that he repeated it often: "There is a school abroad, there is a school in England and in Canada, a school which is perhaps represented on the floor of this Parliament, a school which wants to bring Canada into the vortex of militarism which is the curse and blight of Europe. I am not prepared to endorse any such policy."

Until 1899, peace had been an abstract, moralistic movement. The idea of arbitration as a means to settle international disputes appealed to idealists and businessmen alike.

Canadian resentment of the one-sided 1902 Alaska boundary arbitration might have fostered doubts about peaceful dispute resolution. Still, had war with the United States really been an option? Angry Canadians blamed the British rather than the Americans, swallowed their chagrin, and claimed a moral victory. Laurier's new minister of labour, William Lyon Mackenzie King, was a skilled mediator of workplace disputes. He became a prominent advocate for international arbitration. Talk of arbitration laid the groundwork for a Canadian–American International Joint Commission to resolve transborder water issues. Next came a reciprocity agreement with the United States in 1911. Again, the portents were dangerous. On September 21, 1911, Canadian fear of reciprocity (and Quebec resistance to a Canadian navy) defeated the Laurier Liberals.

Peace activism grew. By 1914, Mackenzie King found fresh work promoting the Canadian–American peace centenary. In March that year, the militarist Canadian Defence League folded. Peace movements announced new adherents.

Suddenly, on August 4, Canada was at war. Plans for the peace centenary collapsed. Proclaiming the Kaiser and German militarism the enemy of peace, most peace activists linked their moral fervour with the British Empire's decision to protect tiny Belgium. Women, Protestant churches and even labour unions rallied to the cause with a zeal some would later find embarrassing. When the Toronto *Globe*'s editor proved a little too moderate, the owners dumped him. This time, the *Star*'s Atkinson showed no such misgivings. Moral reformers supported conscription in 1917 as a logical necessity, and it took the real hardships of wartime life in 1918 to fray the pro-war consensus.

Generally, only Hutterites, Quakers and other sects with a religious commitment to non-violence came through the war with their pacifist principles intact.[1] They and a handful of radicals from secular organizations kept the pre-war faith, enduring denunciation, dismissals, threats and occasional violence. After the war, they gave Canada's peace movement a hard-edged, radical fringe. Optimism about the perfectibility of man was a war casualty, especially in North America. Post-war pacifists linked capitalism with militarism as a cause of war. Hadn't Russian Bolsheviks ended Russia's participation in the Great War? By arming and encouraging the anti-Bolshevik "whites," the Allies had caused the ensuing civil war and famine. Even Canada had sent soldiers to Archangel, Murmansk and Vladivostok. While Bolshevism was too extreme or conspiratorial to hold most peace activists, it acquired an enduring "benefit of the doubt."

Others identified with pro-labour social democracy, whose major Canadian leader, James Shaver Woodsworth, had been a leading wartime pacifist. Fired from his Winnipeg job for his outspoken pacifism and expelled from the Methodist clergy for his radicalism, Woodsworth entered Parliament in 1921. In 1932, he became founding leader of the Co-operative

---

1. The Military Service Act allowed conscientious objectors (COs) to appeal to tribunals on the basis of sectarian pacifism, but tribunals refused to accept some groups, such as the International Bible Students (Jehovah's Witnesses) or the Plymouth Brethren, as denominations. Some military officials enjoyed making martyrs of "conchies," and fellow soldiers administered beatings and freezing showers to COs who refused to drill. Alberta Tory lawyer and future prime minister R. B. Bennett espoused the cause of the war resisters in the courts in 1917–18 and, in a memorable case, forced the Supreme Court to reverse its principles and deny human rights when it refused to nullify the MSA. Quebec voters remembered this in 1930.

Commonwealth Federation (CCF), forebear of the New Democratic Party. His wife, Lucy, joined Laura Jamieson as Canadian leaders of the Women's International League for Peace and Freedom (WILPF, or WIL for short). Woodsworth was too committed to democracy for some pacifists, who ignored the violence of Russia's new soviet government, embraced its anti-capitalist rhetoric, and adopted Communism.

Less radical pacifism revived in post-war Canada, as it had after the Boer War. Enthusiasts welcomed the new League of Nations, the demilitarization of a defeated Germany, and disarmament treaties that cut the strength of major navies in the 1920s.[2] Such idealism might have been strained by viewing the drab-looking diplomats in the League's palace in Geneva or by observing how easily arms inspection in Germany generated paranoia.[3] A naval disarmament treaty that limited major battle fleets to the US and Britain so outraged Japan that it fuelled a militarist putsch and, ultimately, Pearl Harbor. However, pacifists were not analytical and the Great War had fuelled blind anger at war and patriotism. Generals were no longer heroes but butchers; arms manufacturers were "merchants of death." In 1921, a rural Ontario riding chose Agnes Macphail as Canada's first female MP. She promptly led a Canadian delegation to a WIL conference in Washington. In Parliament, she railed against cadet training, hazing at the Royal Military College and the annual militia estimates.

---

2. Idealism or opportunism? Mackenzie King hailed disarmament and cut spending by scrapping the cruiser and destroyers Britain had given Canada for its post-war navy. Two small but new destroyers took their place.

3. Arms inspectors in post-war Germany never quite dispelled the suspicion that industrial chimneys concealed heavy artillery or that toy factories were easily converted to building tanks.

Heading a coalition of westerners and embittered Quebec anti-conscriptionists, Mackenzie King's Liberals were attentive to peace advocates. Only tradition and uncertainty about the new veterans' vote kept military spending in the government estimates, but it was sharply trimmed. Oddly enough, cadet training grew. Ill-paid high school teachers relished a $140 bonus for each ninety cadets they trained, school trustees found drill a cheap substitute for physical education, and even Quebeckers liked a disciplined youth. Despite condemnation, the number of cadets grew from 47,000 in 1914 to 112,000 in 1926, though support dropped in the 1930s. Meanwhile, peace movements multiplied and petitions spread. In 1931, the WIL collected 491,000 Canadian signatures for universal disarmament.

The early 1930s marked the height of inter-war pacifism in Canada. The Depression mocked earlier claims that the Great War would lead to a better world. Anti-war poets, novelists and journalists were in vogue. So were voices promoting radical, even revolutionary, change. Capitalism stood accused of creating misery in peace as well as in war. Yet the Depression years split the broad coalition of peace and reform movements. In 1934, the renowned American theologian Reinhold Niebuhr, a former president of the Fellowship of Reconciliation (FOR), denounced fellow religious liberals and pronounced society, if not individual man, to be intolerably evil. Niebuhr's target was broader than Hitler's Nazism: the peace movement had ignored the Japanese invasion of Manchuria and it would ignore Mussolini's war on Ethiopia. But it was the horrors fostered by the Nazi führer that dissolved pacifism as relentlessly as war had in 1914. The German kaiser might have been a questionable villain, but there was no ambiguity about the horrors of Nazism. Those who were too highly principled to fight Hitler made very few converts.

In the thirties, Canadian consciousness had little space for the outside world, but Franco's assault on Spain's socialist government penetrated and split public opinion. Canadian communists answered a Soviet call and raised a larger contingent for the International Brigades, per capita, than did any country but France. A communist-inspired League for Peace and Freedom met Moscow's demand for a common front against Hitler and Mussolini. Woodsworth's CCF shunned the communists but helped send Dr Norman Bethune's blood transfusion unit to Spain.

By 1939, when pacifists recognized that world war was inevitable, their old lists of members and petition-signers were almost worthless. From an earlier list of three thousand fervent opponents of war, the FOR found only sixty possible contacts.[4] Still, Canada had changed. When war came in September 1939, there were no cheering crowds. When Woodsworth broke with the CCF to oppose the war, his speech was heard by a generally respectful House of Commons. Emotionally ambivalent about the war like most Canadians, Mackenzie King applauded appeasement to the end, prayed that Canada could escape more than minor involvement in a European conflict, and worried that many Canadians shared the views of the frail old CCF leader. In fact, Canadians were more belligerent than their MPs. In the

---

4. Though most of its members were active Christians, FOR in Canada recognized its weakness and proposed to remain broad-based and secular. Its American and British parent organizations firmly insisted on a religious basis, recognizing the malleability of mere liberal convictions.

1940 election, Agnes Macphail lost her seat and Woodsworth almost lost his in Winnipeg North-Centre. Patriotic zeal revived, especially after the fall of France in May 1940, when Britain and Canada stood seemingly alone against Hitler.

Pacifists sought exemption from the National Resources Mobilization Act's home-front conscription. Communists, who had abandoned the peace movement to fight Nazism, switched again in August 1939, after Stalin's pact with Hitler. When communists ordered militants to wreck the war effort, the RCMP swooped. In 1941, history turned again: Hitler invaded Russia and communists were patriots again: some enlisted, others demanded a no-strike pledge from fellow unionists. As "Labour Progressives," the Communist Party gained respectability—at least until 1945, when the party line changed again.

As in 1914, wartime pacifism was left largely to the religious. While radical Doukhobors and Jehovah's Witnesses were unbending, Quakers and Mennonites helped develop forms of alternative service for conscientious objectors. Editors, veterans' groups and assorted patriots raged at those who would not fight, but Ottawa proved reluctant to make martyrs of them unless openly provoked.[5] COs laboured in camps on government projects or handed over most of their wages to the Red Cross for its humanitarian work. Pre-war liberal pacifism largely vanished, save for the lonely members of FOR.

---

5. The pacifist Doukhobors' Sons of Freedom sect benefited for a time from, ironically, a campaign of violence and destruction in response to some young men being held for service: the government found that enforcing the law took more police than it could spare. The less violent Jehovah's Witnesses for a time paid a higher price in confinement and service.

In 1945, the war's final year, issues of peace and war were transformed by nuclear power. "I am become death, the destroyer of worlds": the words of the Hindu *Bhagavad Gita* came to nuclear physicist Robert Oppenheimer after the first atomic bomb exploded at Almagordo in New Mexico. Two other bombs killed over eighty thousand people in the historic Japanese cities of Hiroshima and Nagasaki. More died horribly from the effects of radiation. Peace movements had often claimed that war would destroy civilization. A metaphor had come true. Post-war tests at Bikini Atoll confirmed the multiple layers of devastation released by nuclear explosives. In 1945, nuclear fission bombs delivered the equivalent of twenty kilotons of TNT; by 1950, nuclear fusion or "hydrogen" bombs promised five to twenty megatons, enough to annihilate all of New York, Moscow or Beijing in a few minutes.

The US monopoly on the atomic bomb encouraged the Americans to demobilize and enjoy their victory. When Igor Gouzenko defected in Ottawa in September 1945, he brought Soviet documents that revealed that the top priority for Stalin's spies was breaking the US nuclear monopoly. Part of Moscow's interim defence strategy was to mobilize peace movements against the United States. Peace became an effective front in the Cold War. Who, after all, could deny the horror of the weapons or justify Washington's refusal to accept international constraints on their use?

Americans could answer that a huge Soviet army imposed Communist regimes on Eastern Europe and backed the Communist advance through China. Though the horrors of the Soviet gulags and Nazi concentration camps were all too comparable, sympathizers ignored the evidence, blamed

Stalinist brutality on Russia's immense wartime losses, swallowed the deceits and euphemisms of Soviet propaganda, and focused on the evils of the United States.

Out of a Communist-managed congress in Stockholm in 1948, and Pablo Picasso's stylized peace dove, grew a worldwide post-war peace movement. In Canada, Communist sympathizers and peace advocates made a troubled alliance. Remembering their pre-war alliance with the radical Left, radical pacifists aimed for a neutral, even pro-Soviet Canada. The peace movement's Canadian leader was a former United Church missionary in China, the Rev. J. G. Endicott, who campaigned for peace, Soviet friendship and victory for China's People's Liberation Army. Anyone who found the combination puzzling was dismissed as a "red-baiter" and later as a "McCarthyite," after the demagogic US senator who was as embarrassing to his side as Endicott eventually was to most Canadians.

Nuclear weapons and their cousins in indiscriminate death, chemical and biological warfare, were horrors that anyone would desperately wish to prevent. If, like most Canadians, you lived out of the line of fire, you could imagine yourself immune as long as Ottawa avoided commitments. Yet most Canadians repented of pre-war isolationism. Post-war Canada became almost a compulsive joiner. Canadian officials sought multilateral linkages to balance the inevitable bilateral partnership with the United States. When the United Nations came together in San Francisco, Canadian diplomats ran interference for American concerns. Ottawa saw itself as an architect of the post-colonial Commonwealth and entered the unfamiliar world of overseas aid with the Colombo Plan of 1948. The creation of NATO in 1949 was "providential," as one Canadian diplomat put it, not just as a barrier against Soviet power but also to persuade Washington to heed its cautious European allies. Canada's peace movement deplored the step, not solely because of the movement's Communist mentors nor even because NATO included a fascist-governed Portugal, but because Canada had accepted a role in the like-liest scenario for the next world war.

Thanks to spies and its own research, the USSR had nuclear weapons by the early 1950s. Whatever its pacifist credentials, the Soviet Union marked major holidays with displays of military might in Moscow's Red Square. Likely Cold War scenarios shifted as soon as huge bombers appeared over Moscow, obviously capable of reaching New York, Washington—or Toronto. In 1957, the successful launch of the satellite Sputnik further shattered North American complacency, and huge Soviet missiles began appearing in the Moscow parades. A third world war would include them. Convinced that Moscow was rational enough to understand counterforce strategy, Washington and Ottawa poured money into civil defence, fighter-interceptors, radar surveillance around the continent, and intercontinental ballistic missiles (ICBMs). Meanwhile, a revived peace movement rallied against nuclear weapons testing, deterrence strategies, and the folly of trying to rescue survivors if deterrence failed.

The peace movement found fresh backers. A Mother's Day protest gave birth to the Voice of Women (VOW); campus rallies led to the Combined Universities Campaign for Nuclear Disarmament (CUCND); for a time, traditional and ideological peace organizations were quite outflanked. Howard Green, a First World War veteran and traditional "yellow peril" politician from British Columbia, became John

Diefenbaker's external affairs minister. Devoted to his grand-children and guided by his deputy, Norman Robertson, Green largely espoused the anti-nuclear cause. So did Diefenbaker. He had trusted President Eisenhower, but John F. Kennedy, youthful, charismatic and a Democrat, commanded no such faith. Letters from anti-nuclear activists moved the prime minister. Polls, showing majority support for Kennedy and for standing up to Soviet pressure, did not. Earlier, Diefenbaker had endorsed nuclear warheads for new Canadian weapons. After 1959, Canada's rearmament stalled.

In 1960, Kennedy faced aggressive Soviet threats to block-ade West Berlin. War in Europe suddenly seemed very close. Then the Soviet leaders settled for the Wall that barred East Germans from leaving their "socialist paradise." In October 1962, the Cuban Missile Crisis risked a North American nuclear exchange. After a few tense, even terrifying days, Kennedy could announce that "the other fellow" had blinked. The triumphal applause ignored some Kennedy trade-offs. Canadians soon learned that Diefenbaker had refused to line up with Kennedy or with his own defence officials. The peace movement had made its point.

Did peace activists rally to Diefenbaker as his own party turned on him? No. Members of the peace movement usually preferred the New Democratic Party (NDP), freshly formed from the CCF. Others voted Liberal, though the Liberal leader, Nobel Peace Prize winner Lester B. Pearson, switched sides on the nuclear issue in 1962 to proclaim that he would fulfil Canada's nuclear commitments. Though the 1962 Cuban crisis precipitated a general election and Diefenbaker's defeat, nuclear weapons largely vanished as an issue in the 1963 campaign.

After April 8, Pearson formed a minority government. Americans were soon preoccupied by their war in Vietnam. Canadians had no role in that sad conflict beyond supplying whatever they could sell, from green berets to napalm components. Peace organizations denounced US policy, welcomed Vietnam War draft dodgers and, like other Canadians, enjoyed a dollar which, by the early 1970s, was above par with the US dollar. Peace activists were largely silent in 1968 when Soviet tanks crushed a short-lived Czech democracy. Nor was there audible complaint when Soviet SS-20 intermediate-range missiles (IRBMs) targeted Western European cities. Peace movement outrage began only when NATO proposed to develop and deploy its own IRBMs.

Peace activists found an easier target when Ronald Reagan formed the most right-wing American administration since the 1930s and dubbed an increasingly creaky Soviet regime "the evil empire." As the US and NATO countries resumed an arms race they had largely abandoned in the 1960s and 1970s, peace movements also revived. An increasingly secular and unaligned movement united middle-class professionals, trade unionists, parents and students, ready to embrace a spectrum of tactics from petition-signing and picketing to overt civil disobedience. The 1960s organizations had faded by the 1970s, but in 1976 the Canadian Council of Churches had created Project Ploughshares which, with the help of federal funding, sent interns to the developing world. Conrad Grebel College, a Mennonite institution at the University of Waterloo, provided a link with an old pacifist tradition, and Operation Dismantle, started in 1977, began by seeking signatures for world disarmament and persuading cities to vote themselves "nuclear-free." Operation Dismantle soon found a more local cause when Canada allowed the US to test its cruise missiles over Canada's Siberia-like subarctic terrain.

Toronto, Winnipeg, Vancouver and other cities developed local disarmament coalitions and peace networks, and by 1985 the Canadian Peace Alliance (CPA) reported 350 member organizations and federations, representing 1,500 individual associations. Canadian Physicians for the Prevention of Nuclear War (CPPNW), formed in 1979, claimed one-tenth of Canadian health professionals as members in 1987. Psychologists organized separately to warn of the effect of war-related terror on children. Veterans Against Nuclear War (VANW) felt empowered to pressure National Defence officials. Pierre Trudeau spent his last months as prime minister touring world capitals to preach disarmament, leaving behind a Canadian Institute for Peace and Security (which, however, did not survive the Mulroney government's shut-down of federal think tanks).

In 1989, the Soviet system collapsed. The Berlin Wall came down, the Warsaw Pact dissolved, and the Soviet Union repatriated its occupation forces rather faster than it could find room for them. The huge rearmament burden imposed by Ronald Reagan's government at the expense of social programs had strained the US economy and civil society, but the effort to keep up had crumpled a corrupt and woefully inefficient Communist rival. Mikhail Gorbachev's *glasnost* (enlightenment) and *perestroika* (restructuring) came too late to save deeply demoralized Warsaw Pact regimes.

The Cold War had ended. For a few months, idealists could dream of a better new world, rescued from the horrible risks of great-power rivalry. Then older evils reappeared with renewed virulence—nationalism, greed, aggrandizement. Countries once constrained by one or other of the superpowers were free to revive old quarrels. Iraq, the West's proxy in a war with Iran, made peace and then, in August 1990, invaded tiny, wealthy Kuwait on the claim that it had once been an Iraqi province. Yugoslavia, where Marxist ideology had forced unity on bitterly hostile Balkan nationalities, exploded in savage ethnic massacres. Similar violence dissolved fragile state systems across Africa, from Somalia to Sierra Leone.

Like everyone else, Canada's peace movement took all the credit it could for the wholly unforeseen end of the Cold War. Its condemnation of the Mulroney government's rearmament plans looked prescient. Its approval of peacekeeping persuaded first the Conservatives and then the Liberals to accept more commitments than the shrinking Canadian Forces could sustain. The one-world vision of Henry Wentworth Monk survived better into the new century than the non-violence of Quakers, Mennonites and other sectarian pacifists, and was more appealing than the defensive individ-ualism of the military-industrial ideology.

In the post–Cold War era, targets for an increasingly diverse peace movement were scattered. Peacekeeping, when there was peace to keep, seemed laudable to many, but not all, who opposed militarism. When there was no peace, and military intervention promised to stop ethnic slaughter, how could it be opposed, save by the argument that the final result often seemed little better than what had preceded it? When the United Nations was too weak, as in Rwanda or Bosnia, or too poorly disciplined, as in Sierra Leone, death and suffering increased. Television was the universal, if selective, eyewitness.

Lacking many clear targets, beyond the US govern-ment's national missile defence project and Washington's determination to use its wealth and technological power to militarize space, Canada's peace movement tended to make common cause with environmentalists and to highlight the ecological damage caused by the Cold War arms race. Efforts by the US and Canada to help Russia unload its massive and deadly stockpile of radioactive materials divided environmentalists. Was their relocation an ecological nightmare come true or a vital humanitarian project? Was it really wiser to leave fissionable material where blackmail or bribery could transfer it to a suicidal dictator or a terrorist organization? Such debates were difficult, particularly after 2000, when a few extremists in each movement claimed that a suicidal dictator named George W. Bush had moved into the White House.

In 1991, Canada's peace movement found a target in the Gulf War. Ignoring Iraq's aggression against a sovereign Kuwait, critics claimed that American imperialism had rallied to defend Saudi oil fields from attack, and that Iraqi oil was the real target. The claim was not broadly persuasive but it was sufficient to make Canada one of the most hesitant Gulf War allies. For all his conspicuous loyalty to President George H. W. Bush and American policy, Prime Minister Mulroney kept a low profile even when Canada sent ships and fighter aircraft to the Gulf. Twelve years later, when Bush's son vowed to depose Saddam Hussein and mustered a hundred thousand US troops to invade, Prime Minister Jean Chrétien publicly rebuked his defence minister for hypothesizing that UN approval might not be essential for Canadian support. While opponents of war mustered in major Canadian cities, many and perhaps even most of their fellow citizens had been persuaded that peace-seeking was Canada's natural role in the world.

No one trying to understand defence policy in Canada can ignore the organizing potential of a peace movement based on innocence, righteousness and Canada's remarkably long immunity from danger. Like Canada's military defenders, the peace movement has tended to almost vanish when threats fade, but faithfully reappears when threats soar. Its horror of violence has spoken to an age in which the human capacity for self-annihilation has become a medical and engineering reality.

Can it also develop the sophistication to respond to problems wrapped in ambiguous complexity and to brave necessary dangers?

7

NO LIFE LIKE IT

FOR SOME YEARS, the Canadian Forces led their recruiting drive
with the claim, "No Life Like It." The slogan had a lot of
merit. Military life *is* different. The Canadian Forces like to
speak of a contract with Canada: while obeying lawful orders,
members have an unlimited liability to take life and, when
necessary, to risk their own. Equally, Canada has an unlimited
obligation to provide the best possible weapons and equipment and to compensate members and their families fairly
when things go wrong. Firefighters, police and other public
safety personnel have a similar contract, but they seldom
represent their country against such a variety of armed and
experienced enemies.

Military life may not be wholly unique. Most service
personnel do jobs recognizable in civilian life. They fix
complex machines, they work with computers, they fly
aircraft and navigate ships. Only a minority serve in what
military slang calls "kill trades," such as firing a machine gun,
mortar or anti-tank rocket, and many of them will "re-muster"

into a trade with civvy-street relevance before they plan to end their career. However, being a member of the Canadian Forces is different from civilian life. Members belong to a strict hierarchy, their place visible in a glance at their uniforms. Distinctions between officers and non-commissioned members (NCMs) have feudal roots, and some of the differences reflect a class system few Canadians still accept.

The Canadian Forces should reflect the society they defend, but most members come from small towns and the poorer provinces, places where other jobs are scarce and local values are often more congenial to military life than those of big metropolitan areas like Toronto or Vancouver. Canada's armed forces lead the world in willingness to employ women in any trade or specialty. Canadian women can fight in the infantry, go down in a submarine or fly a CF-18 supersonic jet fighter. Some do; most, so far, don't. The same is true of Canadians from cultures that have traditionally resisted or deplored military service. However, the Canadian Forces have had two hard lessons in why they must reflect their country. A refusal to accept our bilingual reality so discouraged French Canadian recruiting in the two world wars that Canada experienced bitterly divisive conscription crises and overseas forces experienced acute personnel shortages. Although most armies use peacetime to fix their problems, not until 1971 and Prime Minister Pierre Elliott Trudeau's Official Languages Act did the CF commit to operating in both national languages. The grumbling has yet to subside.

A much-debated feature of military life is how to prepare armed forces personnel to meet their liability. How fit, how smart, how stable and how well educated must recruits be? To attract women or under-represented groups, should standards be lowered, or will that stigmatize them? Can psychologists pre-screen for susceptibility to post-traumatic stress disorder (PTSD)? Should they be allowed to try? Between 1939 and 1945 so many volunteers were rejected because of an "S" or stability factor that politicians accused the generals of conspiring to bring on conscription.[1] Yet rates of psychological breakdown in action sometimes exceeded even losses due to physical wounds. Today, even some routine peacekeeping operations have produced PTSD or "Operational Stress Injuries" (OSI) in epidemic proportions.

"Join the Army and Learn a Trade" is an even older recruiting slogan. As mentioned, some naval or military skills are unique to the CF's warlike roles. Canada needs soldiers who can aim and fire a rocket launcher, read the radar screen in a Coyote, load an anti-aircraft missile or calibrate a 155-mm howitzer. Though it costs five million dollars each, and takes years, Canada needs to train fighter pilots. Persuading Canadian women and men to devote their lives to such work is a perennial challenge, particularly since the work requires impressive physical and mental fitness. How many Canadians knowingly seek hardship, demanding discipline and a stressful family life, with perhaps one chance in a lifetime of seeing real war? Service members qualify for a particular military occupational category (MOC). While most MOCs have civilian counterparts, from cooks to instrument mechanics, the Canadian Forces usually has to train its own specialists. This is a costly, time-consuming procedure, but often such training is the reason a member enlisted in the first place.

1. For a fuller discussion, see Terry Copp and Bill McAndrew, *Battle Exhaustion: Soldiers and Psychiatrists in the Canadian Army, 1939–1945* (Montreal & Kingston: McGill-Queen's University Press, 1990).

All CF uniformed members share "basic" training, formerly at Cornwallis, the wartime navy recruit base in Nova Scotia, nowadays at the "Omniplex," a vast building near St-Jean, Quebec. In "basic," recruits master the lore that uniformed soldiers and sailors have needed for centuries, from how to apply a mirror shine to their dress shoes, to whom and how to salute. Recruits learn armed forces jargon for administrative procedures, status and organization. Master corporals, with a maple leaf above their two chevrons, have power; ordinary corporals, with just two chevrons, no longer do. Every aspect of military life is regulated, whether by the National Defence Act and Queen's Regulations or a curt shout from a platoon sergeant. Piling up all the orders, regulations and instructions governing a recruit's life requires a three-metre shelf. Experts insist that the modern CF needs fewer rules, but governments, royal commissioners, administrators, judges and—yes— experts keep on dreaming them up.

More than teaching rules, or how to avoid getting caught, basic training tries to transform recruits from self-interested, rights-conscious individuals into the loyal, dependable parts of a complex military machine. Early on they learn that their new twenty-five-to-thirty-member recruit platoon matters; they don't. Failures and achievements, rewards and punishments depend on the whole platoon. Only platoons win or lose the obstacle race or the drill competition; individual members can't. If Jill or Joe can't yet climb a rope, others had better help or the platoon won't finish the course. If Jack or Jane leaves a messy bed, the whole platoon risks its leave next Saturday.

This sounds tough in a country with an acute case of Charter-based individualism. Charter author Trudeau admired courage and enjoyed adventure but he was no fan of the military. When the Canadian Forces sought a Charter exemption, Trudeau bluntly said no. Few public institutions have fought a harder rearguard battle. The reasons for resistance strike most armed forces veterans as fundamental. Military training prepares men and women to do two unnatural things: to destroy fellow humans and to risk one's own life. Willingness to do both in awful circumstances determines victory.

Why *do* people do it? The answer, consistent over centuries, is that group identification makes the difference. Philosophers and poets used to claim that patriotism or religious faith inspired courage. Aristocrats insisted that courage (theirs, naturally) inspired the troops. Traditionalists argued that valour was based on devotion to the Legion or the Regiment or the Squadron. Soldiers won't die for Canada, an officer told me, but they will do so for the Royal 22e Régiment. Twentieth-century psychologists and sociologists scorned history, got scientific, and discovered that military courage depended on face-to-face groups no bigger than a platoon of twenty to forty members or (preferably) a section of six or eight. When things got tough, an immediate buddy or two made all the difference. What mattered was how you related to the people close to you. In modern spread-out war, only a few comrades actually saw whether you had guts or that you were "yellow." On their own, lost or bereft of pals, soldiers did badly. Because buddies shared hopes, fears and the latest package from home and because, despite orders, they stuck around to patch up your wound, they mattered. It was mutual, and it was true at Second Ypres, on D-Day beaches or on patrol in Bosnia. Loneliness was both a symptom and a cause of "battle exhaustion" or PTSD.

Basic training tries to transform a bunch of self-willed Canadians into something like their group-conscious ancestors. It *is* old-fashioned, ego-bruising and controversial. Inevitably, the Charter-era Canadian Forces have made compromises, partly under political pressure, partly to break out of recruiting ghettos like the Atlantic provinces and small-town and rural Canada. To represent all of Canada, the CF needs young people from big cities and multicultural communities to whom individualism is the Canadian way. The prophets of high-tech, 2020-era warfare insist that fighting will be done by self-starting, individualistic electronic geniuses who can name their own wages in Silicon Valley. How many high-tech Internauts would knowingly sign up for group-first indoctrination? How many want their lives minutely regulated by a three-metre shelf of rules?

Yet when military members control vastly sophisticated weapons with life-and-death power over thousands and even millions of people, surely society requires more disciplined behaviour than can be imposed on mall rats playing space games at a video arcade. Despite what the experts in ethics and law say, some in the CF doubt that self-willed individualists are the "right stuff" for Canada's military. Will they be there when times are tough and dangerous? Will they obey orders that may make sense to a court of inquiry or to Parliament but which sound unreal to service members on the spot—and which could even be fatal?[2]

---

2. Mohawks living near Montreal have their own proud warrior tradition, backed by war memorials for all of Canada's twentieth-century wars. Today many Mohawks do terrifying work, such as building high steel towers in New York. Mohawks want the young men of their community to get military experience. These days, Canadian Forces' "basic" isn't good enough, Dr Taiaiake Alfred of the Kahnewahke reserve told me. Mohawk warriors choose the US Marine Corps boot camp because American Leathernecks make no-nonsense soldiers.

Leadership training, traditionally, meant more of the same, with opportunities for initiative and intellectual initiative. Candidates show their stuff when they stand in front of their own class and give them orders. What is the place of officers, commissioned and non-commissioned? In a free and democratic society, we can hardly argue that being born into certain families makes one a leader, though some militia regiments were run like a family estate. The Prussians who helped the Americans create their military traditions also gave us a pattern. The United States Military Academy (USMA) at West Point trained engineers to build up a raw country, but anyone who survived the four-year ordeal had surely earned some right to lead. The success of West Point–trained officers on both sides of the American Civil War helped make the point. Canada's Royal Military College, which opened in 1876, was modelled on the USMA. Its military training might have been limited and old-fashioned, and the hazing of first-year cadets was sometimes brutal, but no one in Canada did better. RMC ex-cadets had a good opinion of themselves, and others seemed prepared to agree. Officers, in short, qualified for commissions by being better educated and surviving a tougher ordeal than other ranks. If they then kept their subordinates' respect, they could lead. Otherwise, they were tolerated as nuisances—or *not* tolerated.

Killing is barbarous and horrifying. So is being killed. Yet six times in the last century, Canadians wanted people to do it, or at least to go through the motions with sufficient realism that the enemy would fall to its collective knees and apologize. The aftermath of the September 11 attacks showed that many Canadians were eager to send their armed forces to new killing fields, though their only, tragic, losses as of this writing have come from "friendly fire."

How do you train people to kill? Not until lately have we tried to train women to kill, but for men, we have resorted to such old-fashioned ideas as unquestioning obedience, male bonding, class divisions between officers and "non-commissioned members" and uniformity. Experience—the "traditional teachings" we now admire among First Nations—told us that this was how to train men to kill the nation's enemies.

While politicians insisted that our forces had to be "combat ready," General Maurice Baril accepted an even higher priority: that despite women's reluctance to serve, one infantry soldier in five would be a woman. The Somalia inquiry demanded, and the government agreed, that combat troops must devote hours of study to ethical ways of fighting. Here are some issues military ethics classes have to consider:

- You command thirty infantry, deployed to protect a vital bridge from capture. The enemy appears and, after a brief bombardment, advances on the bridge, driving civilian women and children in front of them. Tell us what you do next.
- You command a recruiting unit in a small Canadian city. Tonight is your tenth wedding anniversary and you are getting ready to go to the small surprise party you have organized for your wife and some of the friends you have made in the city. The phone rings. Your sergeant reports that one of your staff has been arrested by the local police and claims to have been roughed up. You know that he is a chronic heavy drinker. What do you do next?
- You are in the last few months of a posting. Your superior is about to sign your annual appraisal. Her assistant (male)

comes to you to complain that she had recently made a sexually suggestive remark in his presence. What action do you take?

There are no correct answers, of course, but the more approved responses strike cynical old me as perhaps just a little unworldly. Preaching ethics is one way of undermining the military's powerful group culture. Your ethical judgement is individual; presumably you are encouraged to value it more highly than the orders from a superior officer or even the interests of your group. Too bad if your side loses or your chums die. Or perhaps, like so much peacetime training, it is all make-believe.

Soldiering is *not* the world's oldest profession, mainly because, for centuries, it was most men's part-time job. Sometimes, when war-fighting technology got too expensive or complicated, the warrior role fell on a minority. In ancient Greece and Rome, where weapons and armour were expensive and military training resembled the physical conditioning of modern athletes, soldiering was reserved for the few free citizens. Slaves did the dirty work, and often they were captives taken in war.

European feudal society was organized so that the labour of a village of serfs supported a full-time knight, complete with his horse, armour, weapons, servants and a ransom should he be unlucky or unskilled enough to be captured. Ransoms were a powerful incentive for poor knights and even common soldiers to risk their lives in the melee of a medieval battle. Knightly chivalry seldom extended to the peasants. Any archers or hangers-on who were captured were slaughtered out of hand. No one ever thought of ransoming them, and the Church frowned on enslaving other Christians.

Of course, not every Athenian citizen or French knight's son wanted to be a warrior. Developing civilization expanded the money supply and offered an alternative: paid substitutes. Mercenaries were cruder characters, rather like motorcycle gang members, who relish money and killing, if not being killed. In civilized societies, like China, pre-Mogul India or Renaissance Italy, the comfortable citizens of affluent communities had no taste for war. The labour market met their need for defenders by supplying barbarians or healthy members of the local underclass. Much as modern capitalists who deal in narcotics recruit biker gangs to do their dirty work, wealthy Italian cities hired bands of *condottieri* to do their fighting in return for cash. Mercenaries migrated from impoverished regions of Europe. Shakespeare's England was one of them, and a splendid statue of Sir John Hawkwood, a wealthy *condottiere*, stands in Venice. "An Italianate Englishman," according to an old saying, "is the devil incarnate." Since *condottieri* had a monopoly of force, they soon used torture and murder to extract wealth from peace-loving citizens. Wealth made them a plague, but they were destroyed when tougher European armies were attracted by Italy's wealth. So, of course, were their employers. If the rich won't defend themselves from the poor, can you count on other poor people to do it? Over the millennia, in China, India, Egypt, Imperial Rome and Renaissance Italy, wealthy people despised soldiering as an arduous and dangerous trade, and then fell victim to their own defencelessness.

Sixteenth-century technology seemed to offer a solution: the gun. Hand-held firearms, after a few centuries of evolution, proved fatal to Hawkwood's mercenary contemporaries. No armour, however elegant, complex or heavy, could resist a small lead ball exploded down a narrow pipe at close range. Even long wooden spears or pikes, held steady by a phalanx of simple peasants, could defeat a charge by expensively equipped and mounted knights. What made pikemen steady? Class helped. Peasants knew their nasty fate if they broke and ran. So did religious faith. By the late 1500s, both Protestants and Catholics faced cruel deaths if captured by fellow Christians. Money worked too. Mountainous Swiss cantons produced thousands of men, Catholic and Protestant, willing to push a pike for money to send home to starving families. During Europe's Thirty Years War, lots of families starved.

Organizing a regiment was a business. In return for an annual payment from the king, colonels organized recruiting, wherein ten captains enlisted a hundred men each for a regiment of a thousand armed, equipped, clothed and paid soldiers. While the colonel often stayed at court, protecting his connections and spending his profits, a "lieutenant colonel"[3] took his place for the dangerous job of fighting battles, wrangling over supplies and preventing his men from deserting. (Government-hating downsizers take note. Who says defence can't be privatized?)

So long as the king had money, colonels and even their captains were happy. The more a colonel could save on clothes, food, pay and other spending, the more he could pocket for himself. One economy was to buy mass-produced

---

3. "Lieutenant" means "place-holder" in old French. "Colonel" comes from *colonna* or column, for the troops marching toward a battle. "Captain" comes from *caput*, the Latin for "head." Captains were subcontractors, finding about a hundred men for their company.

clothing or "uniforms." A French unit, the Régiment Carignan-Salières, may have started the new fashion. Ordered to go to Canada in 1661, the regiment was in rags after fighting the Turks. When the troops showed up in Quebec, all wore brown woolen coats and breeches. Someone in France had sold the colonel an unfashionable dye lot as a "special."[4] The idea caught on. Uniforms became not just a convenience but a preoccupation for tailors, designers and hobbyists. Usually they matched the style of the contemporary dominant military power. Until unification, Canada's three armed services imitated their British counterparts, with some officers even buying their uniforms on Savile Row in London. Now Americans set the style, and all ranks and both genders wear much the same clothing for routine work or combat.

Regiments, colonels, captains and uniforms still exist in Canada's armed forces. So do mixtures of traditions associated with navies, the sea, air forces and flying. Like armies, early navies ran like businesses. Warship crews distinguished between the soldiers who did the fighting under their captain, and a humbler ship's master who had "mastered" such mysteries as setting the sails, getting oars to stroke together or navigating strange seas. Much later, when steam engines displaced sails, engineers were introduced as a crude, grubby subspecies, to be treated with a little awe and much disdain.

As in regiments, the ship's captain recruited his crew, and bought grog and victuals and spars and sails. He even paid

---

4. Much later, when it was formed in 1918 by the combination of Britain's army and navy flying services, the Royal Air Force adopted a stock of surplus blue-grey cloth, once intended for the Czar of Russia's cavalry. The Czar was soon dead, but the RAF set a worldwide fashion in air force uniforms.

from his own pocket for extra gunpowder so that crews could practise shooting their cannons. When his ship captured an enemy vessel, his crew got part of the "prize money," though the captain and his admiral got the lion's share. A lucky, aggressive captain could get very rich. So could a colonel, if he kept costs and casualties down. On land and sea, war was a business. Seamen and soldiers might advance through promotion and prize money, though their pay was often kept far in arrears to discourage desertion. Once paid, most soldiers and sailors spent their tiny fortunes on drink, prostitutes and gambling.

War as a business had the virtues and the vices that nineteenth-century critics discovered in business as a whole. Getting rich was certainly an incentive for colonels and captains alike, but what if an ambitious captain abandoned the fleet to hunt for rich prizes? What if a colonel pared costs so his soldiers starved or froze? Seamen and soldiers were among the most exploited of workers—poorly fed and paid, brutally punished, and often left to beg if they survived sickness and crippling wounds. Not until conscription in Europe and liberalism in Britain and the United States did the appalling conditions of life in the ranks or "below decks" begin to improve. As late as 1916, Canadian military pension regulations dated from the War of 1812. Incomes for soldiers' families depended substantially on patriotic charities.

After Confederation, Canada's defence depended entirely on a part-time, volunteer, community-based militia. That encouraged a version of history that insisted that militia had always defended Canada, from the earliest days of New France, and that regular soldiers, with their Prussian-style discipline, old-fashioned tactics and snobbish officers, merely got in the way. There was some truth to the charge. In New France, underfed regular soldiers, swept up from French seaports, often stayed home and did farm chores while *habitants* under Canadian officers donned snowshoes and raided New England villages. British regulars tended to desert to the United States; locally recruited volunteers seldom did. To this day, regulars spend time fussing over details reservists don't have time for.

In two world wars, Canadian reserve units made possible a dramatic expansion of tiny peacetime forces, not so much by signing up en masse as by providing a cadre of officers and non-commissioned leaders to organize thousands of civilian volunteers. The distinction is important because reserve units like to believe that they mobilized, went to war and did the fighting. In reality, most members could not abandon their jobs and families on a few weeks' notice, and chances are that they would never have joined their unit if that was part of the obligation. In Canada, it never has been. Reservists volunteer to join and, if needed for active service, they must volunteer again. Some, and sometimes many, volunteer. Some can't and don't. This annoys regular force members because they don't have the same choice. If a soldier likes his current job or his wife is expecting their first baby, he may be able to argue his way out of a call to Bosnia or Afghanistan, but it may damage his career.

In the Second World War, the navy's volunteer reserve manned the hundreds of corvettes, frigates and outdated destroyers that escorted convoys and gradually won the Battle of the Atlantic.[5] The army's regiments bore names that showed their affiliations with historic militia units. After the war, battlefield achievements joined a regiment's history. Air force auxiliary squadrons provided pilots for operational squadrons and cadres for the British Commonwealth Air Training Plan (BCATP) and shared in wartime achievements.

The Cold War was different. The Soviet threat endured for decades and had to be met by "forces in being." Instead of a tiny corps of instructors for its reserves, "regulars" became Canada's front line of defence, with a priority claim for whatever weapons and equipment Ottawa would provide. The bitterest moment for the reserves came in 1958 when the Militia was stripped of its operational equipment and training and assigned to "National Survival" duties, which meant rescuing survivors of a nuclear attack. In practical terms, the decision made sense. NATO doctrine insisted that only fully trained and equipped forces "in the front window" would be useful against a Soviet attack. With Cold War armies already mobilized, Canada could not count on the months and years it had taken in 1914 and 1939 to recruit, train and equip its soldiers, sailors and flyers.

By the 1990s, Canada's reserves had dwindled to a quarter of the size of the regular forces. The navy built a class of small

---

5. The Royal Canadian Navy Volunteer Reserve (RCNVR) came from towns and cities across Canada, and usually had little or no maritime experience. They were known as the "Wavy Navy" because RCNVR officers wore their rank in wavy stripes on their cuffs. A much smaller Royal Canadian Navy Reserve (RCNR) was organized from merchant seamen and fishermen who knew lots about ships and the sea but not much about fighting U-boats. RCNR officers wore double strips of wavy stripes. After the war, such distinctions were eliminated and all wore the same uniforms and badges.

coastal warships to meet its responsibility for minesweeping and inshore defence. Reserves took responsibility for these ships and their defensive duties and for control of merchant shipping in time of war. The air force assigned a few squadrons of helicopters to its reserve squadrons, and selected reservists for tasks they could take over in time of need. Communications, now a separate service, found special roles for its reserve members.

Canada's land forces faced the biggest difficulty. Overworked in peace support operations but desperately short of equipment, personnel and training facilities for its regular units, the army looked to the militia to provide junior officers and soldiers to "augment" its ranks. The militia resented relegation to such a role. Its historic regiments were now restricted to a hundred or so soldiers, the size of a small company. Units saw little modern equipment, and their size and constant turnover limited training. Still, militia units often had the political influence and community connections to make themselves heard. The army's harsh realities might not be changed, but they were challenged by prominent honorary colonels, veterans' groups, local mayors and MPs. Added to the rivalries among regular regiments and branches, they made land forces leadership look inept. "Selection and maintenance of the aim," the first principle of war, applies equally to struggles for resources.

Historically, navies and armies depended on a robust class system. "Other ranks" (or the "lower deck" in the navy) were largely filled by the illiterate sons of unskilled workers, farm labourers and the unemployed. Who else would put up with the conditions? The toughest and often the best of them rose to be non-commissioned officers (NCOs). A corporal or leading seaman controlled half a dozen to a dozen subordinates while petty officers and sergeants were second-in-command and often the effective managers of a naval division or an army platoon of twenty to forty subordinates. A few of the ablest NCOs reached the august eminence of chief petty officer or regimental sergeant major. Their status was demonstrated by wearing an officer's uniform.

Non-commissioned officers are the acknowledged core of any military organization. They know all the rules, they manage all significant administration; they could even operate the ship or command a battalion in battle if necessary. One of their harshest duties is covering for officers who may be ignorant and sometimes cowardly or inefficient as well. It was and remains a tricky and testing role, since officers not only earn more than almost anyone in the ranks, however experienced, but they also can usually count on other officers to back them up.

One of Rudyard Kipling's barrack-room ballads referred to "the non-commissioned man" as the "backbone" of the army, and in all services, the word recurs. Their ancestors were the centurions and the tough rear-rank veterans who made the Roman Legion such a powerful force. If there are "professionals" in the armed forces, imbued with its ethos, dedicated to its values and committed to this unusual life, they will be found among the non-commissioned officers. Their leaders are warrant officers (WOs), and the modern CF matches every commander, up to the Chief of the Defence Staff, with a chief warrant officer as both model and representative for all other non-commissioned members. When the Chief Warrant Officer of the Canadian Forces speaks at the Defence Council, the admirals and generals shut up and listen.

As with officers, some NCOs hold their stripes because technical knowledge or skill entitles them to higher status and pay. Some seldom concern themselves with the discipline and performance of others. Some who do have occasionally been reluctant to accept the revolutionary social changes that our times and Canadian Forces policies have imposed on them—bilingualism, female sailors and soldiers and, above all, individual rights under Canada's Charter of Rights and Freedoms. As we shall see, some radical views about future wars and the forces needed to fight them include elimination of the non-commissioned officer category. However, those opinions discount the NCO contribution and its adaptability over centuries of conflict.

The knights of medieval times evolved into "officers and gentlemen." Some studied the evolving profession of arms; most no longer had to, since armies that manoeuvred into line needed generals and staff officers to plan and execute operations, and NCOs to see to discipline. The essential attribute for most junior officers in early modern European armies was exemplary courage. In battle, regimental officers led their men into an attack; in defence, they endured enemy fire with all the sang-froid they could muster. Only when modern weapons forced armies to burrow into the ground and wear uniforms that made them hard to see did junior officers have to become minor tacticians. But so did corporals and sergeants.[6]

---

6. At Vimy Ridge in 1917, Canadian soldiers stumbled on the solution to the terrible impasse of trench warfare. Instead of trying to advance in a rush, as they had at the Somme in 1916, Canadian divisions broke the infantry into small teams and gave them objectives and weapons suited to the problem. The technique demanded good team leaders, and the CEF proved good at finding them. Some teams succeeded, some failed, but the attack flowed through weak points in the enemy line. Eventually the Canadians began calling themselves "The Ever-Victorious Corps." Tanks, guns and airplanes helped too, but not as much as flexible tactics and leaders with initiative.

Until the 1870s, the British Army linked itself with the wealthy propertied class by requiring most officers to purchase their commissions and to buy promotions. After Edward Cardwell, the British Secretary of State for War, abolished "purchase" in 1871, "gentlemanly" standards were upheld, as in Europe and the US, by military academies and selection boards attentive to accents, schools and parental status. Officers' messes, an aristocratic lifestyle and wardrobe, and meagre pay obliged most British officers to have private means or worrisome debts. Canada adapted such old-world customs with embarrassing ease and a few alibis. Officially, militia commissions were reserved for men willing to spend a few months in a military school, buy costly uniforms and transfer their pay to the regimental funds. The policy was not designed to commission penniless farm boys or apprentices. Since Canada's Royal Military College charged fees until 1940 and issued no degree for its four-year course until 1959, cadets usually came from families wealthy enough not to quibble about certification. Very few cadets came from French Canada for a course offered entirely in English in a very British atmosphere. In 1952, the opening of the Collège militaire royal de St-Jean, which included a pre-degree preparatory year, meant that francophone cadets could enter with the eleven years of schooling common in Quebec and the Atlantic provinces.

Even in wartime, social status and education helped to determine officer status. In 1914, would-be CEF officers needed a militia commission and a recommendation from their colonel. Not until 1917 were officers chosen solely from the ranks. In both world wars, high school matriculation or university education made young men eligible for a commission. So did a father's professional status. Military doctors, dentists and veterinarians became officers. In Britain, nurses were not considered ladies, but Laurier's minister of militia, Dr Fred Borden, decided differently. Women who entered nursing, he explained, came from "good families" and would be commissioned.[7] Pre-commissioning training for Canadians included doses of mess etiquette and instruction on "OLQs" (officer-like qualities). Until unification of the services in 1967, Canadian officers were exempt from many punishments inflicted on lower-ranked members, but they could be "cashiered"—dismissed in disgrace—a punishment that repudiated their honour as ladies or gentlemen.

Professional expectations for junior officers grew dramatically during the twentieth century. Naval officers had always been expected to master seamanship and the techniques of navigation; now they had to understand electricity, mechanics and a procession of new and changing technologies. Army lieutenants, once expected to set a brave example, took on technical and tactical responsibilities hitherto left to colonels and generals.

When aircraft became part of modern war only ten years after the Wright brothers flew at Kitty Hawk, flyers were few and reckless. Initially, as British historian Dennis Winters revealed, instructors could not even tell a novice how to get out of a spin. It followed that pilots would be officers, even when they exercised no command greater than their own plane and its small ground crew. When air forces tried to prune

---

7. Nursing sisters ranked with army lieutenants; a matron, in charge of a hospital's nurses, ranked as a captain. The chief matron of all nurses was a major. Even a junior doctor ranked as a captain, and subordination was seldom an issue. Now, of course, gender is no bar to any rank, service or career specialty.

costs and reduce officer-bloat by limiting some of their flyers and other aircrew to non-commissioned ranks, the resulting inequality seemed unjust. Why should one Lancaster bomber have a flying officer at the controls, and another a sergeant, both of them a year out of high school? Finally the wartime RCAF gave its sergeant-pilots commissions; the RAF refused.

The air force example has been richly influential for those who imagine future wars as Nintendo-like deployment of electronically controlled weapons of mass destruction, manoeuvred by computer-competent specialists modelled on the crew member of *Star Trek*'s spaceship. More and more professional or technical positions in the CF have been reserved for commissioned officers who, as social workers, human resources specialists, historians or micro-electronic engineers, never expect to lead troops or risk their lives, but who expect the salaries, status and privileges reserved for a higher caste than those who sleep in bunks, eat in mess halls and drink their beer in canteens. Unification of the armed services underlined distinctions among combatant officers. As Lieutenant General Guy Simonds reminded a parliamentary committee, an air force pilot will usually be alone in the sky when facing the decision to fight or flee; a naval officer may be doing duty in the bowels of a warship when the captain, several decks above, makes that choice. An army platoon commander may be huddled in a muddy ditch with the remnant of her soldiers, trying to figure out how to motivate them to fight and not to flee. All are junior officers, but only the last bears a military officer's traditional responsibility of showing leadership amidst danger.

By the 1990s, one member in five of the CF held a commission, one in four non-commissioned members was a senior non-commissioned officer, and 1 in 400 members was a general or an admiral. Canadian Forces rank-bloat was a reflection of half a century of peacetime careerism, and was partly explained by so-called civilianization in the 1970s. If a civil service director general, ranked as E-1 in the public service, could preside over fifteen subordinates, so could an E-1 brigadier general. Despite the best efforts of Treasury Board watchdogs to stop "classification creep," the pay and status needed to keep clever, talented and expensively trained members in uniform came with higher rank.

Between the 1960s and the 1990s, the traditional military pyramid of ascending rank and power, with a general at the top and lots of privates on the bottom, changed shape. It squeezed into a plump, egg-shaped profile, with fewer privates than corporals, and more captains than lieutenants. At Trafalgar in 1805, Nelson needed lots of hands to swab decks and pass the cannon balls. Modern warships need lots of officers with engineering and computer skills to handle their sophisticated equipment, but shells race up a hoist to the lone gun, and steel decks glisten under an automated sprinkler system. Air force captains pilot forty-six million dollars–worth of CF-18 Hornet, and wonder whether Canada's next fighters will even have space for a pilot amidst the electronics.[8] Only armies still try to line up seven hundred soldiers behind a lieutenant colonel. Could a few dozen well-trained Special Forces do the same job—perhaps with local mercenaries to do the

---

8. They may if Canada buys the latest US-approved F-35 strike fighter at US$100 million each. However, the cost will cause any government to have second and third thoughts. Americans talk about "Aronson's XVIth Law": by 2054 the newest US fighter will absorb the entire US defence budget. It will probably have a "pilot" but he will sit where he can do no harm.

dirty work and the dying? Or should Canada keep its traditional army and volunteer for that role? As we shall see in
Chapter 10, there is a case to be made for this option.

Above the officers are their generals, admirals and, before
1967, air marshals. In both world wars, Canadian commanders brought massive military inexperience—accompanied
sometimes by a saving wealth of pre-war civilian responsibility—to informed decision making. They succeeded provided
they knew their limits and were given a chance to learn. Their
most serious problem, outlined by J. L. Granatstein in *The
Generals*, and easily visible in more recent Canadian Forces
leadership, is long peacetime military experience.

Through the 1980s, three or four times a year I taught
young captains at the former Staff School in Toronto. I also
taught majors, ten years further on in their careers. The
former were bright, challenging and often impressive; the
latter were circumspect, cautious and even deferential. It
could have been me they were afraid of, but I think it was the
paralyzing fear of making an attributable error. Can the battle-
winning attributes of audacity and risk-taking survive the
stifling triviality of peacetime service? As a senior naval
officer told me, in war he would be expected to risk anything
to sink an enemy warship; in peacetime his career might be
ruined if he lost a five hundred–dollar dinghy in a storm. Who
can practise risk-taking in a system governed by a three-metre
shelf of rules and frequent "zero tolerance" for anyone who
makes a mistake?

Most officers are distinguished from NCMs by education,
but even some privates and corporals now have university
degrees. In the 1940s, as minister of national defence,
Brooke Claxton proposed that a university degree be a

prerequisite for a commission in the post-war forces; only between 1995 and 1997, when Doug Young was minister, did it become a rule.[9] However, a diploma can be a symbol without much substance unless the goal is an educated officer corps. Where, after staff college, do Canadian officers study the profession of arms? Claxton opened a National Defence College; few mourned when budget cuts closed it in 1995, because the NDC was a corpse. As a source of intellectual experience or transforming ideas, it had suffocated in the CF's anti-intellectualism. When it was first resurrected as the National Security Studies Course, most students had to perform their day jobs while attending seminars in Toronto. It took a couple of years to liberate full-time students for full-time study. A vital feature of the course is forms of expression. Will senior officers learn to express themselves in plain language?[10]

Canadian commanders, and the retired officers who do much of their lobbying, carry little weight in Ottawa. Do they understand why their concepts seem so irrelevant or why their heavy, Pentagon-style prose identifies them as ritual repeaters? Do they even know other Ottawa policy makers, or meet

---

9. To be fair, many fine officers with little formal education are promoted from the ranks. And a university diploma only hints at the possibility of an education, as any professor knows. Faced with officers desperate for a degree since 1997, some Canadian universities have been flexible beyond principle to cut deals for "life experience" or prior qualifications.

10. The most obvious symptom of any leadership is how it expresses itself. Is the message clear, persuasive and understandable, or is it complex, exhausting and freighted with needless acronyms? Does the prose speak with the authority of active verbs, or does it avoid responsibility through the passive voice? Read any passage of official National Defence prose not filtered through professional scribes at Public Affairs and judge for yourself. Were you stirred or stunned?

them informally? Even when national security issues are headlined at federal government conferences, officers from the George Pearkes Building seem to be invisible and unheard. Postings to National Defence Headquarters (NDHQ) are almost universally resisted because of a legitimate aversion to long hours of bureaucratic irrelevance. With two universities, a wealth of resources and a packed calendar of security intellectuals, Ottawa should be a coveted post-graduate experience for any military professional. NDHQ talks this talk. How about its walk?

8

LIFE CYCLES

ALL HUMANS ARE PREOCCUPIED with the cycle of life. We pass impatiently through childhood and adolescence; we have our earning, and often family, years; we grow old and a little creaky, and we will die. Anyone who has ever owned a car or even a bicycle will understand the life cycle of a machine. It starts shiny, new and full of features that may or may not be useful but all of which add to the salesman's pitch. Used cars lack the glamour and that "new car smell," but they usually work fine if the dealer is honest—and they cost a whole lot less. New or second-hand, all cars lose value as soon as they are driven off the lot. They lose even more, especially in the owners' eyes, when they suffer that first tiny scrape. But their value really tumbles when the new models appear. All at once some handy-dandy new gadget makes *all* the difference.

Of course, over time, a car or bike also starts to need repairs—whether it be to the tires or the transmission or the brakes—especially if you use it a lot. That five thousand-kilometre check-up, when the dealer pays most of the costs, is the last of its kind.

The same things happen to military equipment, be it a big Patrol Frigate launched in the 1990s, a CF-18 Hornet fighter delivered from MacDonnell-Douglas in the early 1980s, or a German Leopard C-1 tank purchased in the 1970s. Equipment starts out as close to the state of the military art as Ottawa feels it can afford. Sooner or later it is surpassed by newer versions or perhaps by a brand new model. Equipment wears out over a period of years, and much faster if it is deployed in combat, perhaps in Kosovo or hunting for blockade runners under broiling Arabian skies.

Crews become more skilful in getting the best out of equipment, and a little Canadian ingenuity may extract higher performance. The CF-18s were chosen partly because they had space to add the latest, most sophisticated equipment, and the American versions really are better than the earlier model. Unfortunately, Canada saw no reason to buy all the new equipment until late in the 1990s. While we were still just about interoperable with the US Air Force, our pilots knew they were flying a plane that was slightly second-rate. And how would you feel if your son, sister or father was facing a deadly enemy in less than the best possible fighter aircraft, tank or warship?

Ships, aircraft and vehicles not only become obsolete over time, but they also wear out. Back in the 1950s, when the world's first jet-powered airliner, the British-built Comet, inexplicably began crashing, we discovered metal fatigue. The painfully expensive solution is to replace stressed metal parts before they break. Sometimes, this is too expensive. Imagine the cost of repairs when military equipment gets very old and the original manufacturer no longer makes the parts. Now you know why the air force was so eager to replace its elderly Sea King and Labrador helicopters.

Just about every specialized piece of military equipment shares the life-cycle problem. Artillery guns are designed to fire so many shells before the barrel becomes too worn to be accurate. In peacetime, gunners may be allowed to fire only a few practice rounds each training year, but the annual toll mounts up. When needed for a real war, guns may be almost worn out. So too may be the engines on tanks and other armoured vehicles. Warships that spend their working lives in the North Atlantic, braving storms and salt water, need thorough refits after a few years. Because this costs a lot of money, a budget-squeezed defence department has lots of reasons to space out refits to longer intervals. Car owners know the temptation—and the likely result. After five or ten years, the repair bill for the pre-winter or spring inspection can be very daunting. So it is for the Canadian Forces, especially when weapons and equipment intended for peacetime training have been pressed into active service in Bosnia, Kosovo or Afghanistan.

Many of us know the feeling when the stove, the fridge and the mixer break down within months of each other. And then comes the frosty morning when the car, too, gives up its ghost. If anyone can remember, weren't they all purchased about the same time? Well, Canada's inventory of military equipment also has come close to a reasonable life span, and some items—notably aircraft and the army's heavy weapons, purchased for Cold War NATO commitments—are long overdue for replacement. Is this a big deal? Surely they are still good enough for peacetime training and if, God forbid, Canada gets into a shooting war, we can buy the best modern equipment from our allies. Didn't we do that in 1914 and 1939?

Well, partly. In 1914, the British reluctantly supplied boots and wagons but they had too few rifles for their own soldiers, let alone to replace Canada's vaunted but deficient Ross rifle. As for the Second World War, our utter lack of modern equipment kept us out of serious fighting until 1942, though wartime propaganda and post-war myths kept this knowledge from most Canadians. In a future war, Ottawa would doubtless turn to the United States, but we would have to wait until the Americans had met their own urgent needs and, since we have no serious arms industry, Canada's forces would make do with castoffs and substitutes.

There is another kind of war weapon that also has a life cycle: the members of the CF themselves. We know something of this from our own lives, be they long or short. Ideally, mentally and physically fit young Canadians enlist in their late teens, close to their peak of physical strength and endurance. Good training and regular exercise extend that physical peak and sharpens mental abilities too, as service members master the skills, knowledge and trades that make them increasingly valuable to their country's defence and security. By age thirty, the ability to survive a sleepless week and still wrestle mountain lions may be waning a bit, but knowledge and experience have transformed a service member into a cool, effective leader and an example to the next generation of CF volunteers. As captains or majors, as sergeants or warrant officers, experienced members provide the CF with a performance edge. Men and women in their thirties kept the CF-18s flying over Kosovo in 1999 and won the 3rd Battalion of the Patricias rave reviews at Kandahar in 2002.

But what about passing the Big forty? It all depends, of course. Fitness can be sustained, experience is piled deeper and there are no age limits on learning. Ideally, this should be the age of Canada's top military leaders. In 1809, when Napoleon turned forty, most of his greatest victories were behind him and his empire was close to its height. The Duke of Wellington took command in Spain at thirty-nine, and had driven the French from the Peninsula by the age of forty-four. Unfortunately, to save pension money, Ottawa now wants senior service members to continue until they are sixty, leaving them twenty years of frustrated ambition to fritter on trivial responsibilities. A better reward for self-denying devotion to national security would be generous education and training benefits for a second civilian career, with the nation continuing to benefit from their ability and experience as members of the reserves.

Age also brings family responsibilities. One of the cruellest burdens Canada puts on service members is the conflict between what US sociologist Mady Segal calls "two greedy institutions." Most of us know the demands of family life, particularly as they fall on mothers. The military can be just as demanding. When TV and newspapers demand that Canada send peacekeepers to some foreign hot spot, and the federal cabinet agrees, Canada's defenders pack their kit and go. The media may record the tearful separations of fathers and mothers from their offspring, but they seldom stick around to check out life as a single parent, or what happens to the children, *both* of whose parents may be service members on deployment. Yet Canadian taxpayers spend a lot of money every year to have the armed forces ready to do their bidding at any hour of the day or night, whether it means patrolling a resentful region of Bosnia or shovelling snow in downtown Toronto to the sneers of the local media.

Family life with young children occurs at almost any adult age, but it is commonest among adults in their late twenties and thirties. And no other single issue is more likely to shorten the "life cycle" of men and women in the services.

When members at the prime of their physical and mental fitness demand release, others have to be found and trained at high cost to take their place. A smart uniform and a nifty Web site won't do it. Mastery of a complex trade and the qualities of a cool NCO demand a huge investment in training and service experience. Doing the best job you can—often with lives depending on you—without adequate training and experience can cause almost as much stress as walking in a field strewn with land mines. In dollar terms, the personnel life-cycle problem for the CF is on a par with replacing obsolete helicopters, worn-out guns and rusted-out warships. It has shaped up as one of the biggest headaches Canada's defence planners face in the twenty-first century. It is part of the reason why the Senate defence committee recommended in 2002 that Canada bring home its armed forces and start refitting, training and organizing them all over again.

Families are both an old problem for the CF and a high-profile new issue. For centuries, the humble status of lower-deck and other-rank service was confirmed by a soldier's own family life.[1] Until Victorian times, a woman allowed to marry a

---

1. A British soldier's wage of a shilling a day was virtually unchanged between Oliver Cromwell's seventeenth-century New Model Army and the First World War in 1914. What changed were "stoppages," deductions for a growing list of benefits such as food, or support for Britain's only veterans' home, the Royal Hospital at Chelsea. One result was that Queen Victoria's private soldiers had less spending money than Queen Anne's.

soldier "on the strength" routinely lived at one end of a crowded barrack room, concealed from a score of other soldiers by a ragged blanket.[2] There she fed and comforted her husband, bore his children, and supported herself by doing laundry or cooking for the other soldiers. Since no one else in the army cared much about feeding soldiers, or washing or mending their clothes, wives performed a vital but unsung service. Should germs or a musket ball lay him low, she nursed him. If he died, a chum usually took his place. When the troops marched, she followed. If the battalion perished in battle, she was booty. Sailors' wives shared their husbands' hammock in port but, when his ship sailed, women were put ashore to manage as best they could. Women were considered bad luck on board any ship.

Victorian sensibilities reacted to such conditions with indignation. Newly built army and navy barracks soon included a few apartments or houses as "married quarters," which were of a quality considered appropriate for penniless families. Canada followed the same pattern. Ottawa allowed pensions for soldiers' widows in 1885, fifteen years before the British, but only in 1916 were mothers, sisters and others we would now think of as dependants considered as part of a soldier's dependent family. One paralyzed father with two soldier sons was ignored while bureaucrats bickered for months over whether a man could be a son's dependant. The poor man died of hunger before a decision was reached! In the

2. The army traditionally limited the number of wives a unit could support to a quota of six per hundred soldiers. Marriage within the quota, or "on the strength," required a captain's permission. Couples who ignored the rules were granted neither pay nor space. When a unit moved overseas, extra women and children were "turned off" at the docks.

1914–18 war, a national charity, the Patriotic Fund, supported "needy" soldiers' families. "Dependants' allowances" were a little more generous in the Second World War.

Conditions for military families, like those for other Canadians, have improved significantly since 1945. A frugal, sober member can become a home-owner, send children to university, and take an occasional holiday abroad. So can civilians with comparable skills and a steady job. Commissioned and non-commissioned members now wear uniforms of identical quality and often eat their meals side by side. Hierarchies matter in military life but, as in the rest of Canadian society, many of the conspicuous symbols of social and class difference have faded into anachronisms. American military sociologist Charles Moskos calls the Canadian Forces the most "postmodern" in the world.

In the 1970s, when the CF adapted the employment conditions for the Public Service of Canada as its model, many traditions of service life vanished. The changes included improvements at the cost of some cherished benefits. As early as 1914, Canada began paying married soldiers a form of marriage allowance, which continued in the Second World War and after. This was a significant advantage because, whatever young couples may believe, two cannot live cheaper than one. No other employer ever subsidized family life in such a way, and the CF were eventually persuaded to end the program in return for more pay for everyone. Married quarters, often poorly maintained but heavily subsidized, had also been part of military family benefits. In the 1970s, rents were adjusted to reflect local rates but upkeep and repairs usually remained a low priority for budget-stressed base administrators.

Military family life can be tough. "The service is wife enough for any man" was an old military slogan. "If you needed a wife," said the US army, "we'd issue her." Traditionally, a spouse was expected to help an officer's career by entertaining, undertaking volunteer work and calling on the wives of his superiors. Imagine that in the twenty-first century! Lower-rank personnel were expected to keep their spouses and offspring under firm discipline, while it was in the family's interests to ensure that the service member performed too. After all, a service member sentenced to detention received no pay.

In the 1950s, Canadian military pay was the highest in the world. That memory even predates a Canadian dollar worth US$1.07. In the 1990s, Ottawa froze all public service wages to trim the federal deficit, and military pay lagged badly. Late in the decade, evidence that service personnel fed their families through food banks and worked after hours delivering pizza persuaded the government to raise lower-rank salaries by up to ten percent. Cost-of-living allowances were introduced for high-cost cities like Victoria and Toronto.

Still, most Canadian families now depend on two adult incomes. So do service families, but many military bases are located in remote, rural or high-unemployment regions where the skills and experience of the non-service spouse often find no market. As short-term residents, military spouses are at a hiring disadvantage to locals. In addition, they often have professional careers that depend on location, seniority and relevant experience. Sacrificing all that to be posted to Gander or Cold Lake can put intolerable stress on a marriage. Like most small communities, CF bases need lots of unpaid volunteer labour that puts nothing in the bank. Nor is it valued or pensionable if married partners split. Increasingly, military members marry each other. The Canadian Forces guarantee that spouses will not be in the same chain of command—but can they always be posted to the same base?

Postings are important, since they fill vacancies, improve career experience, enhance skills through courses, and rotate members through remote, difficult and glamorous locations. Change is always stressful, especially for families with children. The burden of packing, moving, settling, finding schools and hunting for a new job falls heavily on the spouse. Some postings split families for months and even years. A small number of units and military occupations perform the bulk of Canada's peacekeeping and operational duties. Some operations are dangerous and most are uncomfortable. All of them compel families to share the experiences of both single-parenthood and reunification. Stress, conflict and divorce result.

Thanks to Mary Collins, an associate defence minister in the Mulroney era, many bases now include Family Resource Centres, managed by their own family communities but increasingly pressed into bureaucratic conformity by the civilian agency that also provides shopping facilities, insurance coverage and sports and athletics facilities for the CF. Higher pay since 1999 has encouraged service members to move off base, find their own homes and neighbourhoods, and reduce their service ties. Pressure for longer postings and a slower "operations tempo" for the CF would allow families to put down deeper roots—though producing even greater stress if operational needs require future postings and separations.

Like military members, spouses must adapt to the group loyalties powerfully sustained in CF culture. It is perhaps harder for spouses, because most have not spent sixteen weeks of basic training to learn "the system."[3]

In any state, and in a democracy more than others, discipline is the essential quality of any armed force. The civil power—ultimately voters like you and me—gives the orders; the military obeys. Their willingness to do so often depends on discipline. Frankly, like most of us sometimes, sailors or soldiers can be in a bad mood. Some orders seem stupid; politicians give themselves raises and forget that soldiers feel inflation too; no one in the ranks can understand how so-and-so got to be a sergeant or an admiral.

So what. You took the oath; you wear the suit; you do your duty. The National Defence Act requires CF personnel to obey the lawful commands of their superior officers. Superior officers exercise power by authority of the sovereign, acting through elected ministers. Their commissioning scroll lays down the hierarchy, as it has since the reign of King Charles II. This is discipline. Ignore it, even a little, and we are all in danger.

In Canada, there are no exceptions to civil authority. Even the idea of proclaiming martial law in an emergency is alien to our constitution, though many Canadians don't know it. Under our Constitution Act, there is no time when the civil authority yields its power. Yet because of their training and

---

3. Deborah Harrison and Lucie Laliberté, authors of *No Life Like It: Military Wives in Canada,* may recognize some of their observations here. They have been filtered through my own upbringing as a soldier's child, as well as membership in a ministerial committee on social change in the early 1990s and an earlier review of families' political rights. In that role I encountered OSOMM, the Organization of Spouses of Military Members, very much the creation of the dynamic Ms Laliberté.

equipment, and especially because of their discipline, the armed forces are useful in a disaster and utterly essential when public order is challenged.

Even in the crisis Quebec experienced in October 1970 or during the Oka blockade in 1990, governments, legislatures and courts still functioned under the War Measures Act or its successor, the Emergency Act. Like other citizens, a soldier, an airwoman or a police officer must act to protect lives and property, but any such act is subject to law. Killing, even in the line of duty or to save a life, will be investigated and may be judged by the courts. The circumstances may seem quite different months later, when all sides are represented by lawyers, and everyone is much wiser after the event. That can be tough for soldiers or police officers, but they learn about it in their training: it is also a state of affairs that people in many other countries envy.

Discipline in the armed forces raises daily questions. Why wear a gas mask on a stinking hot day? Because that is the weather in which a smart enemy would try chemical weapons. Why salute some twit because he happens to wear an officer's uniform? Why waste fifteen minutes on a checklist when you know your aircraft's crew chief is the best in the squadron? Why risk going on deck in an Atlantic storm just because some petty officer told you to? Why bother taking a prisoner all the way back to the prisoner-of-war cage after he probably killed your best pal? And why not beat up some jerky Somali kid who tried to steal your kit after you came to his wretched country to help save his life?

Discipline is controversial. Vegetius, a Roman historian, thought his empire fell in part because Roman soldiers got tired of carrying their heavy armour and because no one in authority dared force them to do so. Frederick the Great, a pillar of the Enlightenment and friend of Voltaire, thought his soldiers should be more terrified of their officers than of their enemy. Some of Frederick's soldiers were routinely beaten to death for minor offences or shot in batches for desertion. Frederick's Prussian grenadiers set a European example for discipline and military success. Nonetheless, we know that individuals and small groups can fight effectively with little hierarchy or discipline. Native warriors in North America were devout individualists, and ran circles around European-trained soldiers (of course, they eventually lost). Modern guerillas often seem to have some of the same qualities; they usually lose, too.[4] Guerillas who succeed, like General Giap's Vietnamese, find ruthless leaders and a discipline that outshines that of the conventional forces deployed to fight them. Individualism encourages valour, ingenuity and spontaneity, but discipline gives courage some necessary durability. So much of military life is uncomfortable—and even downright dangerous—that most of its practitioners need more than free will and a worthy cause to make them stick at it.

Canadians have always had mixed feelings about discipline. We would love to believe that the *habitants* in the colonial militia could have saved New France if Montcalm had not arrived with his regular troops. For years, Ontario students learned that Upper Canada's brave militia, perhaps inspired by General Isaac Brock, had driven off the Americans in 1812. In the long struggle between Sam Hughes's militia

---

4. The word *guerrilla* is Spanish for "little war" or "la petite guerre"—the phrase our *Canadien* ancestors used for their frontier raids on the Thirteen Colonies. Guerilla warfare is therefore a tautology, but usage seems to legitimate abusage.

amateurism and the Permanent Force professionals, many of us would rather cheer the militia. We envy Australians for their image of "wild colonial boys" in South Africa and the First World War. How dull to discover that Canadians won victories only after they became efficient and disciplined soldiers. Most Canadians are horrified to learn that twenty-two of the twenty-five Canadian soldiers executed in the 1914–18 war died because, in one way or another, they disobeyed orders to stay with their units and fight. We were wiser in 1939–45, when thousands of frightened soldiers were treated for "battle exhaustion"—though their absence made it tough for the soldiers who stayed to fight. More harshly, the air force labelled flyers who backed out of operations as "LMF": loss of moral fibre. Of course, they had abandoned the job of fighting Hitler to their buddies, sometimes at a very awkward moment.

Without discipline—or moral fibre—could Canadians have broken through Hitler's Atlantic Wall on D-Day, flown the missions over France and Germany that made D-Day possible, or fought off waves of attacking Chinese soldiers all night at Kapyong on April 22–23, 1951? Discipline kept troops talking at Oka in 1990 and police pistols holstered during the anti–free trade riots in Quebec City in 2001.

Some traditional ways of instilling discipline now seem very old-fashioned. Saluting commissioned officers or leaping to attention when one of them enters your barracks, responding to shouted commands like an automaton during parade-square drill, or standing stock-still and straight-faced while an instructor bellows sarcastic abuse might suit feudal peasants but not the computer-literate women and men of Canada's modern armed forces. Surely a little open-minded discussion would be more civilized.

Indeed, current policy statements propose that all ranks discuss, in a reassuring, consensual way, Canada's "military ethos." The trouble is that admirals, generals, colonels, warrant officers and sergeants—and especially we civilians whom they serve—also expect infallible discipline. An undisciplined military force is armed and dangerous. Too much of our modern world lives with the menace of military coups and bandit armies. This is not an option Canadians want to discuss in an open-minded way.

Like other threats hinted at in these pages, an uncontrolled military menace will strike Canadians as utterly remote and happily impossible. It follows then that military discipline is not an optional extra but a core assumption in a democracy; more so, perhaps, in a profoundly unmilitary society than in one that trumpets patriotic and militaristic virtues.

9

WHO'S IN CHARGE?

IN MY CAMP BORDEN days back in the 1960s, I shared a course with some officers from Nigeria (including a number of Ibo) and Trinidad. Ottawa had offered to teach them some professional infantry skills, trusting that other lessons of soldiering in a peace-loving democracy would rub off. (We did the same for Warsaw Pact officers in the 1990s.) By the end of the 1960s, the Ibo in the group were mostly dead, victims of their Muslim comrades in the bloody prologue to Nigeria's civil war in the 1970s. The oldest Trinidadian, a charming and funny former schoolteacher, died in a ditch in Port of Spain after taking part in a failed coup.

Canadians live in a hemisphere where almost every country has experienced a military coup, and often many of them. In some countries, military dictatorship has been the norm. In much of Asia and Africa, the barracks is the normal source of government. However primitive, poorly trained and faction-ridden a country's armed forces may be, they have the tools to impose order and organization on their fellow citizens. In the

Western Hemisphere, Canada and the United States are exceptions, but both were shaped, constitutionally, by memories of England's only military dictator, Oliver Cromwell. Our ancestors learned how Cromwell's New Model Army dissolved the "Rump" of the Long Parliament and how, for ten dreary years, Cromwell ruled England as Lord Protector. Among other oppressive measures, he banned the pleasures of Christmas.[1]

No wonder the English welcomed Charles II home to become their "Merry Monarch." When the King and his successors needed soldiers, Parliament agreed, but only if the Army Act was renewed annually. To make sure that officers identified with the wealthy, not with future Cromwells, Parliament insisted that their commissions be bought and sold. The Royal Navy was different. Its efficiency mattered to an island kingdom, officers needed to understand navigation, and when had an admiral ever become a dictator, except in his own fleet? In the Board of Admiralty, civilian and professional leadership mixed.

Better schooled in British constitutional history than their descendants, Confederation-era politicians embraced a parliamentary tradition of civil supremacy over the military and, until 1909, largely left naval matters to the British.[2] British

---

1. In my final year at the Royal Military College, a few cadets kidnapped the speaker of the Model Parliament at Queen's University across the bay, returning him in time for the opening where one "young gentleman" recited Cromwell's dismissive words to the bemused student politicos. I recall no penalty for this lively history lesson.

2. The wisdom of doing so was underlined by the fate of HMS *Charybdis*, an old gunboat offered as a training ship, and foolishly accepted by Ottawa in 1880. A succession of comic and tragic misadventures led to *Charybdis* being towed around from Saint John to Halifax in 1882 and gratefully returned, leaving only bad memories of the problems of Admiralty.

parliamentary practices were embedded in the British North America Act of 1867. But which practices? The fight for "responsible government" in Canada had essentially been a struggle over who distributed government jobs and favours: colonial officials or provincial politicians. The politicians had won and, regardless of party, they were not going back to the bad old days. Moreover, they needed control. Elections were decided not by flacks, hacks and spin doctors but by gratitude. Voters expected politicians to deliver jobs, wharves, post offices, contracts and any other government favours, from military rank to the beef contract for next summer's militia training camp. Then, as now, Canadians hated taxes but they loved public spending. In the 1830s a US president and former general, Andrew Jackson, justified flagrant patronage with a useful slogan: "To the victors belong the spoils." Like most American ideas, the spoils system slid across the Canadian frontier. Gratitude for spoils was the glue that turned the MPs Sir John A. Macdonald called "loose fish" and "shaky fellows" into the loyal partisans needed for stable parliamentary government.

A much younger British tradition, dating only from Victorian times, separated civil and military spheres. Until then, patronage, party lines and aristocratic influence often interfered with British military and even naval discipline, appointments, promotions and other issues of command and control. Colonel John Simcoe thoughtfully named Toronto's main north-south street after George Yonge, the political benefactor who had given him a job as Upper Canada's governor. The Victorians largely removed party politics as a factor in internal management in most departments of government, including the army and navy. Merit, sometimes measured by formal examinations, determined entry. Seniority became the basis of promotion, balanced by performance and qualifications.

Like most reformers, the Victorians admired their handiwork, boasted of its efficiency and fairness, and deplored the corruption and waste of less enlightened regimes. Among those regimes was the crude, corrupt government of Victorian-era Canada. So long as the British managed Canadian defence, politics hardly mattered. Who got colonelcies in the sedentary militia or which volunteer militia units got new red coats made little difference to British officials. Once Canada took over militia administration in 1867, politics began to matter a lot more. The adjutant general of the new Canadian militia, the talented Colonel Patrick McDougall, quit after he was forbidden to discipline Belleville's Major Mackenzie Bowell. Surely, said Bowell, his rights as a newspaper editor and Tory MP outranked McDougall's authority. Disagreements like the one between McDougall and Bowell (who rose to become, respectively, a British general and probably Canada's worst prime minister) would be replayed many times.

In 1872, a Canadian, Colonel Walker Powell, replaced McDougall as adjutant general. An ex–Reform MPP in the United Canadas, Powell lasted in the appointment until 1896. He knew his political ps and qs, but no one pretended that he knew much about soldiering. By 1874, Liberals and Tories had agreed that Canada needed a British officer to command the militia. Delighted to retain some authority over Canada's forces, Britain agreed.

They should have thought again. Only the first British "general officer commanding" (GOC), Sir Edward Selby-Smyth, completed his term, mainly by being agreeable to everyone. After him, ardent reformers alternated with sleepy British veterans eager to enlarge their salary. All became embroiled in conflicts over promotions, appointments or the club-style furores that often exploded within militia regiments. Selby-Smyth's successor, Colonel R. G. A. Luard, had a bad temper and much to provoke it. Fred Middleton's credibility was enhanced by having a French-Canadian wife and by crushing Riel's 1885 rebellion, but his Canadian subordinates complained that he did not get them enough decorations. An inquiry branded him a thief for sending home furs for himself and his political superiors. Colonel Ivor Herbert infuriated militia officers by rebuilding the despised Permanent Force. A bilingual Catholic, he also angered Protestants by praising Quebec's French-speaking militia and urging his staff officers to learn French. Colonel Edward Hutton came to Canada convinced that he had worsted colonial politicians in New South Wales and eager to repeat the feat. His reforming ideas coincided with a rare reforming minister, Laurier's Dr Fred Borden, but Hutton's insistence on monopolizing power and publicity wound up his Canadian career in only two years.

Fresh from glory in South Africa, Lord Dundonald became GOC in 1902. Believing that Canadians were serious about wanting war with the United States over the Alaska boundary, Dundonald would have armed Canada to the teeth. Instead, after two frustrating years of wrestling with Borden, Dundonald openly sided with the Tories on the eve of the 1904 election. Within days, he was on his way home. Most Canadians by then preferred a politician of their own to an arrogant British aristocrat.

Dismal performance in the Boer War persuaded the British to replace their commander-in-chief with an Army Council, bringing ministers, senior staff and officials together in a body modelled on the Navy's Board of Admiralty. Canada followed suit. Major-General Percy Lake, a British officer with Canadian roots and experience, became chief of the general staff (CGS). In 1908, Brigadier General William Otter, a grizzled veteran of the force, became the first Canadian-born CGS, but Lake was promoted to inspector general to outrank him. In theory, more authority now devolved to regional commanders; in practice the Militia Council made the decisions, but only after the minister of militia had approved.

As minister after 1911, Sam Hughes ran the Militia Council like a dictator. Canadian officers knew the dangers of disagreeing with him; a British CGS, Major General Colin Mackenzie, learned by being dismissed. A junior British staff officer, Colonel Willoughby Gwatkin, took his place. A well-educated, civilized man who specialized in ornithology and macaronic verse, Gwatkin sacrificed his career to hold Canada's war effort together during the First World War, and died soon after, presumably from the strain of working with Hughes and his successors. By infinite labour, patience and charm, Gwatkin won the confidence of the wartime government and benefited from Sir Robert Borden's personal contempt for patronage and political pull.[3] By 1919, the war

---

3. Sir Robert Borden's distaste for the "gratitude" principle permeated his 1907 "Halifax Program" and fuelled his personal campaign against the Laurier government. It did not affect his party: throngs of Tories invaded Ottawa in 1911 to claim the "spoils." Borden's chief joy in his wartime Union government was the possibility of a bipartisan bureaucratic reform of the federal civil service, including seniority, classification, competitive examinations and even merit.

had produced enough trained and experienced Canadians that Ottawa felt confident enough to appoint a Canadian.

Civil–military conflicts at militia headquarters were usually trivial. In 1904, Dundonald had exploded because a Liberal cabinet minister from the Eastern Townships refused to let a prominent Tory command a new cavalry regiment. Earlier, Luard had quit after a Tory colonel allegedly cheated with impunity at a rifle match. In 1897, highly publicized disputes in two wealthy city regiments ended with a Liberal colonel upheld in one case and a Tory repudiated in the other. In such cases, there were at least two sides to the argument, but the British general usually insisted that colonial politicians had impugned his authority. For their part, politicians saw political trouble aggravated by an outsider's insensitivity. Hypocrisy is the tribute evil pays to virtue: those involved in a battle used any arguments they needed. Generals pleaded British professional practice and fairness; politicians responded in the name of democracy, Canadian identity or civil supremacy. With rare exceptions, ministers prevailed.

Appointing Canadian-born senior officers made less difference than nationalists might have expected. They were British-trained, pro-British and conscious that British traditions were their model. Given the self-satisfaction of the militia and the innocent idealism of Canada's tiny international affairs community, only the British backed Canadian professionals in seeking military reform in Canada. In 1922, Canada's militia, navy, air service and, briefly, the newly formed RCMP were united in a single Department of National Defence (DND). The minister summed up his goal in words his successors might echo: "a well-organized snappy defence force that will be a credit to Canada without being too expensive." Most historians

describe the ensuing years as a time of stagnant obsolescence.
A new Defence Council provided a forum for claims on a fast-
shrinking defence budget, but no means of resolving disputes
beyond internal negotiations or the fiat of an ill-informed
minister of national defence. As chief of the general staff, Major
General J. H. MacBrien, a bright but acerbic ex-Mountie,
was the overall uniformed boss, but he and three fellow
generals from the old militia department fought the army's
battles. Rear Admiral Walter Hose, chief of the naval staff,
sat alone, though the deputy minister, Georges Desbarats, was
a quiet ally: he had earlier been the navy's deputy minister.
MacBrien relegated the RCAF's senior officer to associate
status. However, unlike the army and navy, the bush-flying
air force made itself useful and popular in peacetime and, on
the rare occasions when strategy was broached, airplanes
filled exciting roles in potential conflicts.

Inter-service conflict could be brutal. Twice between the
wars, the navy faced oblivion. It survived because of Admiral
Hose's bureaucratic skills and the political allies he could
mobilize through his new network of local reserve navy units.
A separate RCAF survived partly because of wartime memories, partly from its useful work, and chiefly because Britain
had a Royal Air Force. When MacBrien left in 1927 to
command the RCMP, he felt as frustrated as any British predecessor. After a year under J. L. Ralston, a fussy, detail-ridden
minister, MacBrien's successor, Major General Andrew
McNaughton, planned to quit. R. B. Bennett's victory in 1930
persuaded McNaughton to stay on, only to endure the
inescapable frustrations of the Great Depression. By 1935,
when his term was up, McNaughton reported that Canada
was a disarmed country. Running the unpopular relief camps

for single men and being deployed to crush strikes had wrecked the army's image and sapped its budget.

Forced to rearm by the world situation in the late 1930s, Mackenzie King ignored his frequently inebriated defence minister, Ian Mackenzie, and his generals and admirals. To King, air power seemed ideal: it covered vast distances and it was unimaginable that cockpits would be filled by conscripts. By 1939, the RCAF had won parity in status with the army and a budgetary edge over both rival services. Canada was less prepared for war than it had been in 1914, but voters hardly noticed. When the military complained of lack of resources, politicians reversed the blame: if pre-war military demands had been more reasonable, the government might have listened to them!

The Second World War did not enhance the fame or political influence of Canada's service chiefs. Brought from retirement to be division, corps and army commander, General McNaughton held, in words cited by *Time* magazine, "the Dagger Pointed at the Heart of Berlin," but he was old, easily distracted and afflicted by the return of his enemy, J. L. Ralston, to run the wartime defence department. In 1943, Ralston and the British forced him out on the pretext of ill-health. When the army's 1944 personnel crisis persuaded Ralston that conscription was needed, McNaughton eagerly accepted Mackenzie King's invitation to supplant Ralston as minister. Only then did McNaughton find that his own charisma was insufficient to persuade NRMA men to volunteer. Mackenzie King found McNaughton to be a broken tool, and voters in Ontario and later in Saskatchewan rejected him as their MP.

Other commanders fared no better. The Battle of the Atlantic was vital to the war effort, but Canada's admirals left it largely to reservists while they tried to build up a "real navy" of cruisers and aircraft carriers. Their minister, Angus L. Macdonald, reserved Nova Scotia's best dockyards to build sophisticated destroyers, not to overhaul convoy escorts. The Ottawa admirals made no protest. Fussing about more training and expensive equipment for convoy escorts was a lower priority in Ottawa than in distant St. John's, where the struggle between convoys and Nazi wolf packs was actually managed. In 1943, after the RCN's inefficiency emerged in a Washington conference on the convoy crisis, admirals were fired, not the minister. Rear Admiral L. W. Murray ably commanded the Northeast Atlantic, the only Canadian sector of the Allied war effort, but he was the scapegoat after his sailors went on an infamous post-victory rampage in Halifax.

The war hardened Mackenzie King's distaste for soldiers. He suspected army generals of yearning for conscription and of bringing it closer by sending too many soldiers overseas and setting "unreasonable" physical and psychological standards for infantry recruits. In fact, like the admirals, army generals had been trained for peace, not war. Professional or part-time, few knew how to use the waiting years in England to train troops efficiently. In battle, as Jack Granatstein and Jack English have separately argued, a few good commanders emerged and taught others.[4] By 1945, Canada's army was as

---

4. See Jack Granatstein, *The Generals: The Canadian Army's Senior Commanders in the Second World War* (Don Mills: Stoddart Publishing, 1993) and Colonel John English, *The Canadian Army and the Normandy Campaign: A Study of Failure in High Command* (New York: Praeger Publishers, 1991).

well led as any other, but the learning costs were high. High casualties ultimately contributed more to the conscription crisis than tests for mental or physical fitness. In 1944, McNaughton allowed King to believe that the generals had "mutinied" when two resigned after failing to persuade conscripts to volunteer. King, converted at last, used the claim to convert anti-conscription ministers.[5] In King's mind, generals had no great claim on Canada's gratitude. General Harry Crerar was Canada's senior operational commander overseas but, beyond a pension, his chief reward after the war was discreet removal from a Hull jail cell and the dropping of drunk-driving charges.

Senior RCAF officers were too busy organizing the two billion–dollar British Commonwealth Air Training Plan (BCATP) to command the few Canadian squadrons sent overseas. Most BCATP graduates went straight to the RAF. Others patrolled for German submarines in the Atlantic or hunted for rare Japanese planes over the Pacific. At war's end, Canada's air force was the fourth largest in the world but, compared to the army's five armoured and infantry divisions, the RCAF had only 6 Group with twelve squadrons. Other Canadian squadrons were scattered through the RAF. RCAF commanders were not found wanting; they were simply not wanted.

King's mixture of contempt and suspicion for his professional military advisors kept them away from most sessions of his war cabinet. An occasional exception was Major General Maurice Pope, the bilingual son of Sir Joseph Pope, Sir John

---

5. Resigning remains an officer's alternative to a hopeless command, though a harsher school favours suicide by walking into enemy fire. In battle, isn't that what soldiers are supposed to do?

A. Macdonald's secretary. The general had inherited his mother's French tongue and his father's political sense. Almost alone in Ottawa, Pope anticipated the long-term consequences of the Ogdensburg Agreement: Canadians, he predicted, would have to do a lot more in future to persuade Americans that they were defending themselves. When Winston Churchill and Franklin Roosevelt came to Quebec City in 1943 and in 1944, to plot Allied strategy, Mackenzie King wanted no role beyond a photo opportunity; Canadian brass hats, he believed, would contribute little to Allied strategy, and that little would be paid for in Canadian lives. Economic concerns were different. American and British generals decided where Canadians would die, but Ottawa diplomats devised what they called a "functional" principle to determine when Canada's interests really mattered. Grain exports, refugees or exchange rates involved Canada's national interests; strategy, tactics and the deployment of Canadian ships, troops or aircraft did not.

In 1945, all three Canadian services planned post-war forces that ignored government—and public—expectations of full demobilization, drastic cost-cutting and, perhaps, something "snappy." The Cold War forced a compromise. With fifty thousand full-time members out of a population of thirteen million, Canada's post-war armed forces reached ten times their 1939 strength, but they were still far short of even the minimum expectations in staff plans. Pre-war rivalries resumed. The post-war chiefs of staff included Air Marshal Wilf Curtis, a First World War flyer and pre-war commander of Toronto's auxiliary RCAF squadron; Vice Admiral Hugh Grant, a cadet at the original Royal Canadian Naval College and wartime captain of a British cruiser; and Lieutenant

General Charles Foulkes, a mediocre divisional commander chosen over Lieutenant General Guy Simonds for the sound reason that he had more political sense. University-trained and attuned to Ottawa's cross-currents, Foulkes outperformed his rivals.

In 1947, when lawyer and ex-CEF sergeant Brooke Claxton moved from the Department of Health and Welfare to become minister of national defence, he matched Fred Borden in reform ambitions. Exasperated by endless inter-service bickering, he promoted Foulkes to be chief of the chiefs of staff committee (CCOS) and Canada's first peacetime general. He also reorganized the three rambling wartime temporary buildings that housed NDHQ: instead of a rival service for each building, each housed a distinct function—operations, personnel and material. By 1950, thanks to Claxton, Canada was well on its way to a unified rank and pay scale, and a single medical service. A new National Defence Act gave Canada a tri-service system of military law. Then the Korean War intervened, NATO commitments followed and Claxton was soon too busy overseeing and justifying Canada's first peacetime mobilization to pursue his reforming vision.

Needless to say, service chiefs deplored Claxton's vision. Such rivalries were tiresome, but normal in most countries and virulent in the United States. Washington's Pentagon was a vast five-sided arena for the struggles of the US Army, the Navy, a new US Air Force and the historic United States Marine Corps. Canadian chiefs of staff soon found American allies and more powerful backing for their inter-service struggles than Whitehall had provided. Moreover, despite creating a chief in Foulkes, Claxton left the defence minister accessible to each service chief.

Ottawa's deference to Britain faded fast after 1945, but its politicians and civil servants were almost eager to gratify their new American allies. In early 1951, when US General Dwight D. Eisenhower pleaded for quick NATO contributions, Canada's services responded from memory. Having adopted the American-designed but Montreal-built F-86 as its front-line fighter, it made logistical and technological sense for the RCAF to fly with the Americans. As CCOS, Foulkes urged a similar affiliation for the army. Guy Simonds, Foulkes's successor as army CGS, vigorously disagreed. His personal experience with the British had been entirely satisfactory and, he hinted, they were much more careful with soldiers' lives than were the Americans.[6] Reluctant to put all the eggs of Canada's NATO commitment in an American basket, Ottawa diplomats and politicians backed Simonds. As for the RCN, its commanders resumed the one wartime role that had gained them a positive image: Canada's warships would battle Soviet submarines in the North Atlantic. In NATO, Canada's three services split into three separate and distinct operational directions.

The early 1950s were halcyon days for Canada's defenders—though halcyon times are known only in retrospect. Rearmament soon absorbed up to 40 percent of federal spending—4.6 percent of the gross national product. Canadians serving with NATO had weapons, equipment and skills good enough to win inter-allied competitions. National prosperity made it all seem affordable. The Soviet threat was never delivered but neither did it fade; it grew and evolved. New

6. Simonds was British-born and, in the eyes of Field Marshal Bernard Montgomery, Canada's only competent field commander. Praise from abroad almost always impresses Canadians.

weapons replaced old ones. Nuclear-powered submarines could stay underwater for months, rendering obsolete most existing means of detection. Intercontinental bombers flew at stratospheric heights and close to the speed of sound. When Avro's twin-engine subsonic CF-100 interceptor appeared, it was promptly dubbed the Clunk and immediately scheduled for replacement by the supersonic CF-105 (the Arrow). Tactical nuclear weapons transformed the battlefield.[7] To survive, armies needed rockets, armoured personnel carriers and tolerance for military and civilian mega-casualties. A few professionals wondered whether such a war might be a little insane. Most refused to let theory affect their plans.

In 1957, Canadians elected John Diefenbaker as prime minister and confirmed the choice by a 1958 landslide. The Tory platform had something for almost everyone, from the elderly to the armed forces. The new defence minister, Major General George Pearkes, a 1917 Victoria Cross winner, had quit Pacific Command in 1944 as one of McNaughton's "mutineers." He endorsed most of NDHQ's dreams, including nuclear warheads for army rockets, nuclear depth charges for the fleet and nuclear missiles for the air force. Like most new prime ministers, Diefenbaker inherited troubles, ranging from Canada's worst recession since the 1930s to soaring costs and no export sales for the CF-105 Arrow. Higher pensions for the elderly and expanded unemployment insurance payments

---

7. A book by Harvard professor Henry Kissinger claimed that tactical nuclear weapons (smaller than the twenty-kiloton Hiroshima bomb) made traditional war possible again. Even with vast dispersion and all-terrain mobility, such a war would annihilate whole battalions and devastate vast acreages, but NATO (and Warsaw Pact) commanders insisted that such wars were winnable—with the right weapons.

coincided with fast-shrinking revenues. Faced with a similar cash crunch, the British and Americans cancelled several costly weapons programs. So did Diefenbaker. On "Black Friday"—February 20, 1959—the Arrow died. Within minutes, Avro fired seventeen thousand workers. Some headed south to US aerospace programs. A myth of the world's greatest aircraft was born.

Later, philosopher George Grant would describe Diefenbaker as the last hope for Canada's independence. But faced with real choices, Grant's hero had quailed. Canada's military dependence on the US was cemented by the purchase of the Voodoo interceptor and ineffective Bomarc missiles. A mutual defence procurement agreement encouraged US-owned branch plants to open in Canada.

By the late 1950s, public opinion about defence began shifting. Had the West's robust response forestalled Soviet aggression? Or was the Cold War born out of right-wing propaganda? Predictably, the Reverend J. G. Endicott and the Canadian Peace Congress had denounced NATO, German rearmament and any other policy deplored by Moscow. Any critic of defence was likely to be labelled a Soviet apologist, but the disastrous miscarriage of US nuclear testing at Bikini Atoll in 1954 raised major scientific and public concerns about radiation and its deadly consequences. New voices entered the debate. What was more patriotic than concern about threats to the health of babies? The Voice of Women (VOW) mobilized eminently respectable middle-class women in the name of nuclear disarmament. The Canadian Committee for the Control of Radiation Hazards (CCCRH) initially refused to consider any form of disarmament until it was pushed hard. Protestant churches, labour unions and university students borrowed symbols and slogans from British and American anti-nuclear movements to mobilize pressure.

Canadians should have been concerned. Bomarcs, Voodoos or CF-100s in the RCAF sector of North American air defence covered Toronto and Montreal as well as New York and Philadelphia. In the name of National Survival, Ottawa did its best to publicize the awful consequences of a war that might have been triggered in 1960 by Allied insistence on keeping a garrison in West Berlin or by a 1961 Soviet decision to send missiles to defend its new Cuban ally, Fidel Castro. In any serious nuclear exchange between the USSR and the United States, millions of Canadians would have sickened or died from radioactive fallout. Was Berlin or Cuba sufficient reason for Canadians to die or Canada to be devastated?

The answer from most Canadians in a time of crisis was to have faith in their leaders and hope for the best. It had usually worked, especially if the leaders were foreign. Canadians had trusted David Lloyd George in 1917, Winston Churchill and Franklin Roosevelt in 1940, and Harry Truman in 1950. Faith in Robert Borden or William Lyon Mackenzie King was more muted. What about John Diefenbaker? In 1957, the Tory leader had campaigned as a Cold Warrior, pledging to roll back the Iron Curtain to liberate captive nations. As prime minister, he had utter faith in President Eisenhower, the wartime "Ike." Defence spending fell from $1.8 billion in 1957 to $1.5 billion in 1960, but Pearkes's nuclear acquisitions seemed to remain on track. Then Diefenbaker noted the strident public criticism and grew evasive. The Bomarc, he insisted, used a conventional warhead—though reporters soon discovered that no such warheads existed. When Bomarc bases opened near North Bay, Ontario, and La Macaza, Quebec, anti-nuclear groups raged, unaware that the "nuclear" missiles stood on guard with sand-filled warheads. In the absence of an agreement, their armament stayed in the United States. The new external affairs secretary, Howard Green, reinforced Diefenbaker's caution. A BC Tory, Green changed in old age into a peace-loving idealist, like his undersecretary, Norman Robertson.

In 1960, American voters chose John Fitzgerald Kennedy (JFK), a younger war hero who alarmed Diefenbaker by responding boldly to Soviet challenges in Berlin and Cuba. When the Cold War heated up, Diefenbaker blamed Kennedy; in a notorious note, JFK described Dief as a "son of a bitch." The climax came in October 1962. Were Washington's smudgy aerial photos of missile sites sufficient evidence to risk nuclear war? As President Kennedy went eyeball-to-eyeball with Soviet premier Nikita Khrushchev and US media coverage of the crisis captivated the public, Canada's ministers debated for two days about whether to approve a NORAD decision to move to an alert just short of war. Suddenly, the Soviet missile-carrying ships changed course. Everyone took a breath. And shouted and raged. What had Ottawa done? Had Canada left the United States unprotected? Not quite. An admiral in Halifax had ordered RCN warships to fill gaps left by American ships. RCAF fighters had staged their own standby. Pearkes's successor, Doug Harkness, had ignored Dief, cancelled leave and approved local orders. (Months later, he quit.)

Canada's role pleased neutralists and disarmers, though Diefenbaker got little credit from them. Other Canadians insisted that this was not how allies behaved. Many Canadians admired Kennedy's aggressive style; others identified with the aging prairie populist. On January 4, 1963, NATO's retiring commander, General Lauris Norstad, visited

Ottawa and told journalists that Canada *had* adopted a nuclear role. Had Diefenbaker lied? Lester Pearson, as Liberal leader, shared Diefenbaker's misgivings but his handlers watched public opinion. Invited to the White House as a Nobel Peace Prize winner, Pearson emerged to announce that he would respect Canada's current alliance pledges until he could negotiate others. In the 1963 election, all parties played down the defence issue. When anti-nuclear rowdies disrupted Pearson's meetings, respectable peace advocates told them to behave. On April 8, Pearson won enough seats to form a minority government.

The Liberal victory, however muted, flattened the peace and anti-nuclear movements: they had simply not delivered the votes. Defence debates continued, but on very different lines. As defence minister, Pearson chose his pro-nuclear former defence critic, Paul Hellyer. Like other kids, the young Hellyer had wanted to fly, but in 1944, Flight Cadet Hellyer's dream dissolved when a pilot surplus converted him into a resentful army anti-tank gunner. He did not forget. Like Claxton in 1947, Hellyer had an agenda: reform of National Defence would be his springboard into Pearson's job.

Reform was needed. Instead of the clear direction other ministers received from a deputy minister, defence ministers got three or more sets of advice, each suspiciously self-serving. Neither Foulkes nor his successor, Air Chief Marshal Frank Miller, had the authority as CCOS to impose unified policy. In the 1940s, Claxton had started to build a single integrated defence structure; Hellyer would finish the job and get the credit. He inherited an asset. Diefenbaker had invited a consultant to apply business wisdom to government structures. J. Grant Glassco reported that National Defence was a mess of overlapping and extravagant services, linked by hundreds of useless inter-service committees. Memories of the Cuban crisis also helped Hellyer. While Tory politicians dithered, the brass had acted. Perhaps they were right, but what if the politicians had been Liberal?

In March 1964, Hellyer delivered the first defence white paper since 1949. He pleased Pearson: peacekeeping was now Canada's top priority. Hellyer also kept Canada firmly committed to NATO and NORAD, leaving home defence at the bottom of the list. In his budget plans, Pearson pledged a steady two billion dollars a year for defence, too little to modernize its 1950s-era weapons. Finding the necessary capital depended on efficiency-based savings. In July 1964, the three service staffs at NDHQ "stood up" as a single Canadian Forces Headquarters (CFHQ) under a chief of defence staff (CDS). A year later, the three services were integrated as the newly named Canadian Forces (CF), with six (later seven) functional commands, each reporting to the CDS. In 1966, scores of camps, stations and land-based ships became thirty-nine Canadian Forces Bases (CFB).

Despite inevitable confusion and complaints, integration worked well. Canada had made changes other armed forces would adopt decades later. Senior commanders took on new jobs, but the three services somehow survived. What worried them more than temporary chaos were words in the white paper that outsiders scarcely noticed: Hellyer had also promised "a single unified defence force." What did he mean? Hellyer's views had evolved since the trashing of his youthful dreams. He absorbed a casual remark by General Simonds that Canada needed a kind of "marine corps" to meet its varied commitments. He heard complaints from clerks, mechanics and technicians that they were second-class members, "purple people," excluded from the three fighting services and denied pay and promotions to match their civilian counterparts. He also bridled at criticism from senior officers who quit only after they were promoted.[8] He resented that colleagues and media treated his achievements as useful but boring: reshaping head office hardly earns headlines.

When the first CDS, General Miller, quit, his successor became Hellyer's chief ally in managing unification. General Jean-Victor Allard had commanded brigades in northwest Europe in 1945 and Korea in 1952–53, and even a British division in Germany. He accepted unification as a lawful order, a personal challenge and an overdue opportunity to rid the Canadian Forces of their British look.

Hellyer needed help. Unification preoccupied Parliament in 1967, Canada's centennial year. Though generals and admirals were unsympathetic witnesses, Hellyer looked merely stubborn. Conservatives filibustered against change. Hellyer's colleagues found unification issues trivial and cosmetic and pressed their own projects. Hellyer *was* stubborn but, for Liberals and their NDP allies, underlying the debate was the issue of civil supremacy. The minister had to prevail. Armed with closure, on April 25, 1967, he did.

Unification was not worth the fuss. It imposed a common green uniform, modelled on that of the US Air Force, which, wearers complained, made them look like bus drivers.[9] Robbed

---

8. Hellyer's reforms coincided with the compulsory retirement of many Second World War veterans at the age of fifty-five. Hellyer noted that few who quit did so without gaining a step in rank and a better pension. Replacements were easy to find.

9. In fact, it was modelled on the basic dress uniform of the USAF, a semi-conscious colonial homage.

of traditional navy blue uniforms, sailors made even less flattering comparisons. Under the green cloth, little changed. Whatever General Simonds had meant by his reference to marines, units of the new "environments" operated as they had before—separately. Canada's NATO land and air contingents now reported as "Canadian Forces Europe" (CFE), but trained independently. An air environment helicopter pilot might fly reconnaissance missions for an armoured regiment or land on the heaving quarterdeck of a destroyer. Most pilots still flew fighters or transport planes. Peacekeeping operations needed signallers, clerks, cooks or technicians from any service background, but a single environment dominated most operations. And no other country followed Hellyer's lead.[10]

Hellyer's image of stubbornness doomed his hope of succeeding Pearson as party leader. Instead, the Liberals chose Pierre Elliott Trudeau and swept the 1968 election. Trudeau's individualism made him no friend of traditional military values. In 1963, he had voted NDP rather than follow Pearson's nuclear switch, and his misgivings about the Cold War and NATO persisted. A chief of defence staff might have been a powerful advisor for Canada's prime minister, but at most Trudeau saw his top general a few times a year. Military expertise had no place in the cabinet "seminars" where Trudeau formulated policy. On April 3, 1969, Trudeau announced a reversal of Pearson's defence priorities and the cancellation of Hellyer's pledge that savings would pay for new equipment. Drastic cuts followed. Bases closed. NATO

---

10. When distinct navy, army and air force uniforms returned with Brian Mulroney's government in 1985, many CF personnel again complained. Why revive an old fuss and wreck the uniformity most units could now achieve only with the common green?

commitments were cancelled and then partially restored. The army's brigade was halved and transferred to Lahr, a small Wurtemburg town within the American zone. Cutting twenty thousand members from the CF eliminated five famous regiments activated by Simonds in the 1950s. Hellyer had proposed to double capital spending; the Trudeau cuts left a mere twelve or thirteen percent for new or renovated weapons. Some of it was wasted. After a costly refit, the navy scrapped HMCS *Bonaventure*, its only aircraft carrier, because it no longer had enough sailors to crew the ship. Voters were shocked at the miscalculation.

Was Trudeau to blame? No, he argued, admirals had refitted the *Bonaventure* and generals had bought unnecessary CFO-5 fighters; he forget to mention that politicians had forced the issue because the plane would be built in Montreal. In response to the criticism, Trudeau's latest defence minister, Donald S. Macdonald, ordered a management review group (MRG) to study his department. The MRG's mood was unsympathetic: after Vietnam, war could be obsolete, generals and admirals were anachronisms, and business methods were the best way to run anything. Integration and unification had failed because they left the military in charge: civilianization, with a deputy minister in charge, would be better. As usual, reforms stopped short of the ideal. After 1974, the deputy minister and the CDS would be equals at the head of a "defence team" of uniformed and civilian employees.[11] Civil

---

11. The rivalry between deputy minister and military commander dated back to early days in the militia department, and generally settled into military control of policy and civil control of spending. Now the two were in the same box in the organizational chart. Observers noted that Ottawa civil service veterans had a lot more leverage than an outsider fresh from Halifax, Saint-Hubert or Winnipeg.

service terms replaced military titles: the chief of personnel became an assistant deputy minister, human resources, military, or ADM (HR-Mil). Some ADMs were generals or admirals, others were civilians. Throughout the new-style NDHQ, civil–military integration was under way.

Civilianization changed more than either of Hellyer's reforms did, and in the succeeding years it has been modified only slightly. Top brass proliferated to match the generous rank structure of the civil service. In the new "defence team," military and civil service conditions were equalized. Old privileges of rank, from staff cars to batmen, faded fast. If a director general drove his own car, why did a commodore need a chauffeur? Logic, a powerful if selective feature of Trudeau-style government, dictated changes. Civilianization ended some old benefits of military life, such as subsidized rent for married quarters or Canadian Forces schools for dependants on bases. Why, the argument went, should service members and their families suffer burdens—or enjoy benefits—denied to public servants? In the 1970s, the benefits as well as the constraints of military life seemed anomalous. Were the changes compatible with the special obligations Canada demanded from its uniformed defenders? Time might tell.

Civilianization affected the professional culture of military commanders, who now had no direct experience of war and no prospect of it. Could anyone learn war through computer simulations and war-gaming? And who got to the top? Bilingualism and fair shares were Trudeau-era values in Ottawa. Was it the turn of a rare francophone admiral or an anglophone but bilingual air force general? An eloquent British admiral, Sir John Fisher, once warned that the Empire would be lost because it was "Buggins's turn." Fisher believed in favouritism because he believed he could identify talent.

Should talent count for more than loyalty and experience? Without a war, who could judge war-fighting ability?

What was merit? Did it merely coincide with those who filled the right jobs, attended crucial courses, pleased patrons and, above all, avoided the "shadows" that always worry selection boards? Shadows fell on officers who took risks, made mistakes, challenged orthodoxy, embarrassed superiors or cleaned up messes left by others. Such behaviour might suggest courage and character, but it also hinted at trouble-making. Peacetime advancement came to smooth, attractive officers with well-managed careers. Some critics alleged that Canada's regular regiments selected favourites and consciously advanced them in their own interest, but tribal behaviour was not limited to the army. What about officers slighted or over-looked by the tribal chiefs?

The Hellyer and Macdonald changes did not make National Defence easier to manage. Competing services fought even harder as budgets shrank. Army, navy and air force might be banished terms, but "Air," "Land Forces" and "Maritime" commands re-emerged in the late 1970s. A single air command gave the air force renewed identity. "Black hats" from the old Armoured Corps[12] rejoiced when Chancellor Schmidt of West Germany squeezed a contract for German-built Leopard tanks from Prime Minister Trudeau. The decision guaranteed their branch another twenty years. After much delay, American concerns about Canada's contribution to both NORAD and NATO led in 1980 to a four billion–dollar contract for 147 McDonnell-

---

12. Armoured Corps personnel have worn black berets since 1919, when the post-war Royal Tank Regiment formalized the black cotton mechanic's "bonnets" they had worn to protect their hair from flying grease and oil.

Douglas F-18 Hornets. Though no service contributed more to Trudeau's "Priority One" for sovereignty and home defence, the navy slid into obsolescence, perhaps because no ally espoused its newly limited role in protecting coastal waters from foreign overfishing.

The election of the Mulroney government in 1984 owed something to voter suspicions that Trudeau had neglected defence. The Conservatives moved quickly to provide three distinct uniforms, to restore the Canadian brigade in Europe and to provide the navy with six, and then twelve, powerful new "patrol frigates." In 1987, an ambitious young defence minister, Perrin Beatty, published a defence white paper embodying the Reagan White House vision of Soviet imperial menace. He even urged his generals and admirals to add their professional voices to the defence debate. The rapid unravelling of the Soviet Union promptly unravelled the white paper's assumptions. Beatty's successors, persuaded by their service advisors, pretended that nothing had happened. One Beatty successor, Marcel Masse, echoed his generals' claim that Canadians had not earned a new peace dividend; they had enjoyed one for years.

The strain of the post–Cold War era and Canada's forty billion–dollar annual budget deficit revived inter-service rivalries. Vice Admiral Charles Thomas retired to denounce General John DeChastelain, the CDS, for trying to maintain combat capability in all three services instead of favouring the navy and air force. Jean Chrétien's Liberals, elected in 1993, upheld DeChastelain by promising forces fit to fight "alongside the best against the best," and then chopped defence

spending by about a third. The 1990s became as uncomfortable a decade in Canadian civil–military relations as any in
the twentieth century.

In the 1940s, Jean Chrétien's working-class father had
ignored majority opinion in Shawinigan and Quebec and
supported conscription. His son inherited his father's stubborn
patriotism but he shared French Canada's mistrust of military
institutions and their proponents. While the Canadian Forces
complained of shrinking budgets and obsolete equipment, the
prime minister saw sixty thousand men and women sharing
the single largest item in the federal budget. He also saw a
post-1990 world in need of peacekeepers. Neither the prime
minister nor most military leaders fully recognized the social
revolution under way in a military organization in the grip of
Charter-inspired change. A succession of defence ministers
failed to reconcile the divergent perspectives.

Throughout the Cold War, Washington, NATO, NORAD
and occasionally Canada's political leaders had determined
Canadian defence priorities and military strategy. The people
in charge of Canada's armed forces did little original strategic
or tactical thinking, perhaps because military thinking had
seemed inappropriate for the armed forces of a junior and
democratically governed ally. In the 1990s, Lieutenant
General Roméo Dallaire argued, there was an interval when
Canadians could have developed their own view of the world.
Dallaire, eager to develop that view, experienced the fate of
being both hero of the Rwanda tragedy and its most highly
placed psychological casualty. Who else in the Canadian
Forces would see the need, have the vision to provide it, and
the courage, in an era of porridgy and acronymic prose, to
convey it in plain language?

In 1994, Jean Chrétien's government had announced a defence policy, and then cut it to ribbons to achieve deficit reduction. Critics occasionally suggested a new policy, but usually as an adaptation of Pentagon orthodoxy. If God knew what to expect in a new decade, She didn't have the patience to explain it to Canada's high command or its political masters. One consequence of the Al Qaeda bombings on September 11, 2001, was to place the Americans once again in firm control of Canadian military thinking. The directives from the White House and Pentagon might sometimes seem misguided, even foolish, and often irrelevant to Canada, but they possessed an authority that even the most civilian of politicians and the most nationalist of commanders could not ignore.

10

FUTURES

ANYONE WHO HAS READ THIS FAR will know my suspicion of forecasting. This has been a self-inflicted wound to my career because most people believe that the only practical use for historians is to tell us what is going to happen. Nowhere is this more true than in the study of war. Starting with the Prussians, every general's staff studied old wars in the hope of preparing their generals for the next war. Where else could they find out what worked in war-making, even when bullets replaced arrows, horses gave way to steam engines, and telephones and wireless sets replaced old-fashioned hollering?

Military futures matter in peacetime because that is when both weapons and warriors are developed. The American victory over the Japanese navy at Midway in 1942 depended on aircraft carriers authorized years before Franklin Delano Roosevelt was elected president in 1932. A tough infantry sergeant who knows how to fight and how to make others fight can take up to fifteen years to train, though the British now claim they can do it in ten years. Canada's Royal Military

College graduates lieutenants and navy sub-lieutenants after a tightly packed four-year program (though cadets from Quebec or the Atlantic provinces who finished high school in eleven years need an extra year). Much of their professional training starts after graduation. An eighteen-year-old who enters RMC with the dream of flying a supersonic fighter can spend ten years training before she or he flies with a CF-18 squadron.

Defence decisions can take forever. When Diefenbaker stopped the Avro Arrow program in 1958, never again would Canada build a supersonic fighter aircraft.[1] Wiping out the design team that produced our City class patrol frigates may mean the same for Canada's hope of building future warships. Abandoning tanks dissolves hard-earned Canadian expertise in armoured warfare. What if Canadian soldiers ever face sophisticated tanks again? On the other hand, do we mourn Canadian military horsemanship or feats of shooting with the old Ross rifle? Life is lived now and tomorrow, not yesterday. Get with it, say the futurists. Get it right, say the rest of us.

Forecasting is tough work and the Department of National Defence has a poor record. In 1949, Brooke Claxton's white paper confronted the Cold War threat by giving top priority to Canada's own defence. A year later, Canada was frantically raising forces to defend South Korea and, by 1951, Western Europe. The 1964 white paper emphasized peacekeeping, but no serious new peacekeeping involvements occurred. By 1972, Canada's home defence again became "Priority One." Why? Each statement dutifully adopted the preferences of the prime minister of the day, not Canada's defence needs. The

---

1. In 2002, even the United States decided that it could afford only one contractor, Lockheed-Martin, to develop the successor to the CF-18.

1987 white paper was designed to please Prime Minister Mulroney by endorsing US President Ronald Reagan's "evil empire" view of the Soviet Union. By ignoring Soviet *glasnost* or détente, the prophetic shortfall added to jokes about "military intelligence." To be fair, the Liberals' 1994 white paper made sensible forecasts about the violent nineties, but its recommendations utterly ignored Canada's fiscal crisis. By demanding more than a sensible government could afford, the 1994 paper achieved instant irrelevance. When defence critics demand a new white paper, they may only want to embarrass the authors.[2]

Prediction is frustrating and unreliable—but inevitable. If we won't make choices, time makes them for us. The passage of time is as inevitable as death and taxes. As we have seen, ships, aircraft and vehicles wear out. So do their crews. Repair bills mount, reliability shrinks, and some cold day, the engine won't even turn over. I have now reached an age at which my body gives me warning signals I never noticed before. A few years ago I met a search and rescue (SAR) crew at Comox, BC, rolling out their 1958-vintage Labrador helicopter. They were flying up a stormy coast to hunt for an overdue fishing boat. Safe? Sure, hours of maintenance and careful crew checks saw to that, but, as a crew member reminded me, a long thin rod linked the forward rotor blades to the engine in the rear. If it were to snap, the aircraft would fall like a stone.

Planning would have replaced his helicopter that year, 1995. Taming the deficit was a higher priority. Had defence

---

2. Demands for a new white paper appear in defence critiques sponsored by the Institute for Research on Public Policy in Montreal and the C. D. Howe Institute in Toronto, not to mention the Calgary-based Centre for Military and Strategic Studies.

planning in 1994 ignored Canada's financial condition? Should it now ignore the competing claims of agriculture, decaying urban infrastructure, health care for an aging population, and the environment, not to mention world hunger and poverty? If so, the next Canadian defence review will be as myopic as its predecessors, and as irrelevant.[3]

Using the past to foretell the future runs into familiar problems. First, we remember only part of the past—most often the parts that make us feel good. The whole story may be too embarrassing, boring and long, but the missing details may make a big difference. Second, making analogies, as I did above, tells only part of the story. Bullets, for example, are a huge improvement on arrows but they have problems too. Unlike arrows, they demand precise manufacturing. A .300 calibre bullet won't work in a .303 calibre rifle. And human ingenuity can usually outsmart both prophets and technologies. Until September 11, 2001, did anyone realize that an airliner with a full load of fuel might be the ideal weapon to destroy a hundred-plus-storey office building?

Generals and admirals, like stockbrokers, are desperate to know the future. For two generations after 1945, the puzzle seemed straightforward. The Third World War would pit the United States against the Soviet Union, each joined by its respective allies. The struggle would resemble the Second World War, plus nuclear weapons. If the Soviets often had an edge in missiles, tanks and submarines, the US was far ahead

---

3. Professor David Bercuson, the principal author of *To Secure a Nation: Canadian Defence and Security in the 21st Century* (Calgary: Centre for Military and Strategic Studies, University of Calgary, 2002), insists that he has no intention of costing his proposals since all of them matter. Even highly intelligent lobbyists feel immune from tough choices.

in computers, aircraft and a huge array of electronic sensors that kept an eye on the vast, secretive Soviet system. When President Reagan cranked up the American war machine in the 1980s, Soviet Marshal Nikolai Olgarkov tried to get his side to measure up. Instead, to general astonishment, the Soviet economy and its military system sputtered and collapsed.

In 1990, after two generations of nervous stability, the world entered a new but bewildering era. Instead of peace, prosperity and happiness funded by "peace dividends" from reduced defence spending, the world passed through one of the bloodiest decades in the twentieth century as conflicts forgotten by the rest of the world burst into flames. From Armenia to Azerbaijan, from Croatia to Cambodia, humans slaughtered each other. Earlier, we saw the impact of this period on Canada's armed forces. Canadians might note that the American experience was similar. After the Gulf War, the US cut a third of its military personnel and a hundred billion dollars in defence spending. During the Cold War, US forces had deployed overseas ten times; between 1989 and 1999, they took on thirty-six foreign missions. Though Canadian Forces may complain about their "operational tempo," the Americans invented the term. In both countries, defence forces faced governments with other priorities such as high taxes and serious indebtedness.

Combining new technologies and appropriate tactics for future battlefields has often given one side in a conflict its margin of victory. History suggests that challengers do it better than champions. Thanks to wars with the Scots, English kings realized that peasant archers with longbows could penetrate a knight's chain mail armour, devastating French chivalry and giving the weaker country famous victories from Crécy to Agincourt. Organized in deep columns of infantry, and buoyed by revolutionary *élan*, the ragged, ill-trained troops of the French Republic smashed into the straight lines of their monarchist opponents and rolled them up, saving the Revolution and later giving Napoleon his victory edge. In 1939–40, blitzkrieg tactics, linking tanks and dive bombers by wireless radio, gave Hitler vengeance for Germany's defeat in 1918. In their time, these were some of many revolutions in the way of making war.

When Americans talk of an "RMA"—a revolution in military affairs—they think they have the answer for future triumphs. What is RMA? Here is the definition *The Economist* offered its readers, courtesy of the Rand Corporation: "[A] paradigm shift in the nature and conduct of military operations which either renders obsolete or irrelevant one or more competencies in a dominant player or creates one or more new competencies in some dimension of warfare, or both."[4]

After humble bowmen began knocking them off, being an armoured knight lost some of its glamour and lots of its value. All the tools that made blitzkrieg possible in 1940 existed in 1918; the trick was to improve and combine them. American-style RMA doctrines grew out of the digital and space technologies that have dominated US research funding since the 1950s. Techniques that put astronauts on the moon and produced the World Wide Web have transformed the way Americans have waged war since 1989, from the Gulf to Afghanistan. They may also have rendered obsolete most of the weapons in the Cold War arsenal.

---

4. *The Economist*, vol. 364, no. 8282, 20 July 2002.

RMA enthusiasts bubble with the acronym C4IST (command, control, computers, communication, intelligence, surveillance and targeting). The C4IST philosophy is embodied in the massively fortified Battle Information Centre (BIC) that Boeing has built for the US Army in Anaheim, California. Three huge screens dominate a large room. They are controlled by three vast consoles and, thanks to satellite technology, can display the world or any part of it, down to the view of a very mean street from a video camera mounted in an infantry soldier's helmet. Using a vast array of information from every imaginable source, a duty officer can zero in on anything suspicious, from a village in the Sahara Desert to a factory gate in Pyongyang, North Korea. The data suppliers include big airborne warning and control system (AWACS) planes, nimbler unmanned aerial vehicles (UAVs) and perhaps an occasional spy in a trench coat.

The urgent need to know what was happening in the highly secretive Cold War Soviet Union led the US to develop a huge lead in surveillance technology. Once a target is identified, computers feed in extra data. Weapon systems, scattered around the world to avoid becoming a target, are networked and alerted. On the commander's decision, perhaps checked out with the White House, a single, suitable missile may be on its way from anywhere that can reach the target. Many US pilots remember how their buddies died trying to knock out a key bridge in Korea or Vietnam. Now the military strategists believe that a single precision-guided missile or an unmanned combat air vehicle (UCAV) can do the job the first time—or smash shut Al Qaeda caves in Tora Bora or atomize Saddam Hussein in his Baghdad lair. And, enthusiasts boast, few Americans will come home in body bags—unless they were treacherously playing with the "bad guys."

RMA includes every imaginable computer application, from global positioning systems (GPS) to sorting billions of megabytes of information. Remote sensors on pilotless aircraft flash real time pictures of the battle space. Robot scanners detect vehicles and weapons and report electronic signatures from transmitters and even telltale road dust from a moving vehicle. Computers absorb vast quantities of input and transform it into information for suitably trained field commanders. RMA-style communications can link President Bush to an infantry squad leader in a Salvadorean jungle. RMA extends to every kind of programming, from directing precision-guided missiles to their targets to giving up-to-the-minute reports on target status. If a busload of schoolchildren drops in for a friendly visit to an enemy missile base, a well-served commander could abort or delay the base's planned destruction—or reconfirm it, because this is the seventieth busload that day!

RMA's most revolutionary claim is that it takes the guess-work out of warfare, from the precise location of key targets to the battle plans of the enemy generals and admirals. Throughout history, commanders have complained about the "fog of war" and worried about what the enemy was doing "on the other side of the hill." Airplanes helped a little. In 1914, a French pilot won the Battle of the Marne and perhaps the First World War by reporting that the German armies were passing in front of Paris, not behind it. RMA techniques would have warned French generals even faster. Indeed, data overload may trouble the high command as much as the earlier dearth of information. RMA enthusiasts have an answer: better training, computers and algorithms reduce the guesswork and the doubts. Machinery, not staff arguments, provide the alternatives and the arguments pro and con.

Today, as usual, experience shapes future threats. The asymmetric war of the past decade, in which the enemies were non-state organizations, or failed states or ones close to collapse, now seems to stretch far into the future. Asymmetric war pitted Al Qaeda against the United States and pro-Western governments in the Islamic world, the IRA against the British army, FARC against the Colombian armed forces, Tamil Tigers against Sri Lanka, and Hamas and Hezbollah against the Israeli Defence Forces (IDF). Asymmetric war may have targeted Australian holidaymakers in Bali and a miniature United Nations of workers in the World Trade Center. It utterly ignores the two-century struggle to "civilize" war, including the Hague and Geneva conventions for the rights of prisoners, medical personnel, prisoners of war and innocent civilians.

Key strategies in asymmetric war include targeting vulnerable people and encouraging the more powerful adversary to make enemies and outrage public opinion by slaughtering innocent people. When a jet fighter killed a terrorist leader with a five-hundred-kilogram bomb, Israelis felt victorious. Hamas made sure the world's media learned that Israel's bomb had also killed or injured a hundred neighbours, some of them babes in arms. It was not a good day for Israel. The British remember Bloody Sunday—January 30, 1972—when paratroopers stopped an illegal march by killing thirteen unarmed Catholics in Londonderry, Northern Ireland, escalating the latest round of the "Troubles." Asymmetric warfare is not for the faint of heart.

RMA techniques seem especially appropriate for the asymmetric and rogue-state threats that have replaced the Cold War as the main challenge to the US and its allies. The promised combination of global reach, precision targeting, minimum personnel and minimum US casualties captivated Bill Clinton's Democrats as much as George Bush's Republicans. The Pentagon, faced with further cuts if it failed to adjust to political realities, responded more eagerly than the individual, traditionally minded armed services it tries to manage, but each service found something new to do. Robbed of the blue-water threat of an enemy battle fleet or a submarine threat to the sea lanes, the US Navy adapted to fighting near "littorals" or coastlines, with missile-equipped anti-aircraft cruisers to guard its aircraft carriers and a new destroyer adapted to deliver shore bombardment. Embarrassed by the US Army's immobility in the Gulf and Kosovo, chief of staff General Eric Shinseki fought his fellow generals to replace heavy tanks and self-propelled howitzers with air-portable "light brigades" and the equipment to back them. The US Air Force created "Aerospace Expeditionary Forces" and contracted for a lion's share of the RMA surveillance commitment. Even the US Marine Corps, long committed to fight anywhere, bid for new helicopters, though it stuck by its heavy tanks.

For almost a century, military forces have been measured in what current jargon calls "platforms"—tanks, bombers, battleships, fighters, submarines, aircraft carriers and artillery guns. Platforms do no harm themselves; they carry the bombs, shells, rockets and torpedoes that do the damage. Nonetheless, the platform becomes the target. Aircraft carriers and their three to five thousand crew members are highly vulnerable to missile attack. So are tanks, self-propelled heavy artillery, missile sites and most other forms of military hardware. Air and naval bases, vital for the repair and maintenance of sophisticated weapons, cannot easily be rolled up and hidden. Nor, for that matter, can the fabulous BIC in Anaheim. Even a hugely protected facility in southern California might not be an impossible target for terrorists who could bomb the Pentagon and the World Trade Center in the same hour.

The idea of RMA deserves tough criticism. Innovators are seldom modest or straightforward about the shortcomings of their dream. Selling the new technology gives high-tech firms a great chance to recoup fortunes lost in the dot-com debacle. Plenty of folks are dazzled by electronic wizardry. Others are reluctant to ask stupid-sounding questions about technologies their teenaged children understand better than they do; who wants to be portrayed as an old fogey fighting the last war over again? Do we trust admirals and generals to reach sound conclusions? Military leaders usually learned their profession in their youth, and got promoted because of enthusiastic orthodoxy. In the US and Canadian military systems, RMA is now part of the orthodoxy.

Still, the US and its allies are staking their security on some very bold claims. Enthusiastic innovators almost always oversell their product and are seldom on hand when trouble starts. The rapid pace of change in computer technology and programs betrays current inadequacies as well as future potential. Transforming war into a kind of high-stakes video game, with few risks to the players, strikes many people as a great bargain. Punishing an enemy, with impunity for the good guys, sounds as good as Hollywood. Aren't our soldiers' lives valuable?

Armed forces brass have different instincts. Some of them are self-interested. Any admiral who ever commanded a giant aircraft carrier or cruiser had trouble seeing the navy's future in the *Arsenal*, a giant, missile-studded semi-submersible barge, with enough stealth technology to escape radar. The US Navy sank that program in 1997. The US Air Force, though the chief advocate of RMA as the logical extension of its high-tech approach to war, bridles at pilotless aircraft. How can its members play a heroic role unless they are pilots, flying dangerous missions?[5]

Generals who trained all their careers to fight Soviet tank armies fought hard for the Abrams tank and Crusader artillery systems because they seemed to be the best weapons ever devised for such a war. But how could you get them to Kosovo, Afghanistan or Iraq in a few crucial days? Now the US Army is committed to buying twenty-tonne "Future Combat System" (FCS) armoured vehicles, which have yet to be built. Soldiers, who do most of the dying in any war, may not be happy, but they have to argue with Donald Rumsfeld, President Bush's war secretary. In 2002, I visited Arnhem, in the Netherlands, where in October 1944 a superb British airborne division had unexpectedly run into a weary, under-

---

5. The Afghanistan War built the reputation of unmanned air vehicles (UAVs) and unmanned combat air vehicles (UCAVs). The Global Hawk, built by Teledyne Ryan, is a high-altitude, long-endurance (HALE) UAV. It resembles a corporate jet in size and can fly over a target for twenty-four hours at sixty-five thousand feet, too high for current enemy missiles or fighters to reach. General Atomic's Predator UCAV flies low and fires missiles. Competing models are in progress thanks to US$1.5 billion in research funds. Meanwhile, keeping humans alive and competent at high altitude and huge speeds drives the price of new fighter aircraft toward US$1 billion each.

strength German panzer division. It was no contest. I came away wondering how the new American light brigades would fare if they ever faced an enemy with real tanks and heavy guns. Count on it that Secretary Rumsfeld won't be there.

Claims for RMA have grown in each of the wars the United States has helped wage since 1989, from the Gulf War in 1990–91 through Bosnia in 1995, Kosovo in 1999 and Afghanistan in 2001–02. While allied aircraft pounded Baghdad with little resistance, they did a better job preparing for the armoured assault that ended the war. Failure to bomb Saddam Hussein out of power was blamed on a lack of precision-guided missiles (PGMs).[6] When Bosnian Serbs massacred five thousand Muslims at Srbrenica in 1995, NATO forces replaced UN peacekeepers, and the US organized an RMA-style air attack. After Serbian leader Slobodan Milosevic abandoned his Bosnian allies, US envoy Richard Holbrooke gave bombing the credit. He ignored the impact of a simultaneous Croatian invasion of key Serb territory. Did Holbrooke's claim persuade NATO to expect similar quick success in 1999 for a US-led bomber offensive? When fighter-bombers took off from Aviano to save Albanians in Kosovo, their bombing campaign lasted for months, not days. Kosovars survived mainly as refugees, and NATO had to switch to plan B. RMA proponents had excuses, from bad winter weather to Russian backing for Milosevic. When Russian backing ended, Milosevic gave up. However, RMA met its

---

6. Only one in ten of the bombs and missiles used in the Gulf War had precision guidance, compared to ninety percent of those used in Afghanistan. PGMs are really a dumb old bomb with a neat electronic inertial guidance attachment to help them stay on target. Unfortunately, in 2003, PGMs are still not yet smart enough to distinguish a suitably equipped decoy from the real target.

political test: by keeping their planes above the ceiling for Serb missiles, US pilots survived.[7] Was preserving Kosovar lives less of a priority?

George W. Bush's war in Afghanistan suited a US administration utterly committed to RMA and the rapid transformation of American armed forces to new technology.[8] As Afghanistan was targeted and a battle plan was compiled at an operational headquarters in Tampa, Florida, US carrier task forces converged on the Arabian Sea to launch assaults on Taliban and Al Qaeda targets. Contingents of US Special Forces landed by helicopter to support Uzbek-dominated rebels and direct fire on their Afghan government opponents. UAVs reported enemy movements and activities to Tampa, and low-flying UACVs thundered missiles at air defence targets. Bases made available by nervous Gulf states and neighbouring Uzbekistan and Tajikistan allowed army and air force deployment. When CNN could report satisfying columns of smoke rising from Taliban and Al Qaeda bases in the Afghan mountains, fears of a costly Rudyard Kipling–style war in the hills subsided, and almost everybody could come home alive. Four Canadian soldiers, victims of US Air Force "friendly fire," were among the sad exceptions.

Critics of RMA read history differently. What happened, they ask, to the original Gulf War plan to destroy Saddam

---

7. A French pilot whose aircraft dropped below the ceiling fell victim to Serb missiles.

8. *Transformation* is a Rumsfeld-era buzzword for adapting each US service to RMA-style warfare, with an emphasis on getting to anywhere in the world to destroy America's enemies. Each service is expected to "transform" itself into small, efficient, globally mobile forces, with light equipment robust enough to destroy the kind of opponents Americans have faced since 1989.

Hussein rather than his country? A dozen years later, he was still in place. The final massive bombing in 1991 left Iraqi conscripts with little will to fight, but Saddam's elite Revolutionary Guard seemed to escape intact. In 1995, a successful Croatian and Bosnian invasion of Serb territory shook Slobodan Milosevic. Four years later, months of NATO bombing demolished less than a quarter of Milosevic's tanks and armoured carriers, leaving his troops plenty of time to make the Kosovars suffer. NATO needed a plan B, but planning delays as well as Albanian roads kept NATO forces far from battle. In Afghanistan, some kind of war continues as I write, with little hard evidence of enemy losses or of the fate of Osama bin Laden. Lacking an exit strategy, American forces are stranded among restive hosts in a nasty climate. Come to think of it, isn't that how those Kiplingesque wars got started?[9]

That's not how the White House or most of the US Congress sees what happened. Nothing succeeds like a proclaimed success, and RMA transformation has become the model not just for US forces but also for their allies. Canadian Forces policy stresses interoperability with US counterparts and, if Ottawa can find the cash, transformation will become part of the CF's future too. Most of NATO's European allies were sidelined in Kosovo and Afghanistan, because their aircraft could not match the speed, altitude and sophisticated

---

9. The first Anglo-Afghan war began triumphantly in 1839, but in 1842 a Dr Bryden, lone survivor of Lord Elphinstone's army of eighteen thousand, rode his donkey back through the Khyber Pass. The British soon recaptured Kabul and then withdrew. In 1879, a British envoy and his escort were slaughtered in Kabul and British troops were beaten at Maiwand. Sir Frederick Roberts recaptured Afghanistan but Britain again withdrew. Fighting continued for decades.

communications demanded by USAF strategists. Most European countries spend more on defence than does Canada, but their forces have suffered similar post-1990s rust-out. Many European governments are making the costly transition from conscription to volunteer professional forces. They also face more resistance from Greens, Socialists and taxpayers if they expand defence spending. Europeans also have a smaller base of RMA-style technology, and US laws on military security and corporate practices leave little room or incentive for significant technical transfers, even to allies. The British, Europe's most effective armed forces, with an older, more trusted relationship to the US, are partial exceptions.

Not all possible threats to the US come from terrorists or "rogue states." One contingency that helped persuade the US in the 1990s to keep forces sufficient for two Gulf-style wars was the threat to its main Asian client state, Taiwan. Taiwanese pressure for sovereign status provokes regular threats of invasion from mainland China, which defines Taiwan as a Chinese province. With a billion people, vast territory and a substantial People's Liberation Army (PLA), the People's Republic of China (PRC) comes closer to superpower rivalry with the US than any other country. Many futurists see China as the next great ruler of the world, though most of them have had to delay their projections several times. While the country's coastal provinces have prospered under cautious state adventures in capitalism, corruption has prospered too. Meanwhile, China's interior provinces have experienced bitter levels of poverty. Critics believe that the PLA, heavily dependent for its funding on China's industrial empire, may itself have been corrupted by *binshan* or soldier-businessmen. Whatever China's military strength, developing

RMA seems a rational US military response to any challenge from the PRC's large but technologically underdeveloped armed forces.

In June 1999, General Maurice Baril, then chief of the Canadian defence staff, presented *Shaping the Future of Canadian Defence: A Strategy for 2020*. In the wake of the Kosovo campaign, interoperability was the fifth of Baril's eight objectives, but its importance would only grow. *Defence 2020* built on over half a century of developing links with US forces. Political advantages matched the military benefits. Ties to the Americans always worry Canadian nationalists and socialists, but such links may not reopen the French–English divide that grew dangerously during the long Canadian relationship with Britain. In an era of Quebec separatism, French Canada's pro-Americanism is a powerful lever in Ottawa.

Keeping up with the Americans has also been the best argument National Defence ever found to loosen up a share of taxpayers' dollars, and that case has worked overtime since September 11, 2001. Not only were many Canadians embarrassed that their forces could not measure up to American military standards, but they also worried about US retaliation if Canada did not pull its weight in President Bush's war. Even politicians who routinely ignore National Defence Headquarters heard from constituents and the media. Finally, and fundamentally, Canadians have real difficulty imagining an international situation in which their forces would perform independently. From the Boer War to Afghanistan, Canada's foreign campaigns have fitted into alliance wars. So have Canada's armed forces. Far away in the Antipodes, Australians were essentially on their own when they faced Indonesians in East Timor, absorbing a few hundred Canadian soldiers as part of the operation. Canadians have not yet played such a role themselves: interoperability is our historical pattern.

The arguments that make RMA technology attractive to the Pentagon apply almost equally to Canada. Defence systems based on limited personnel, low casualties, global reach and frontier science and technology are a good fit for Canadians who have no plans to join the military, much less die in battle, and who believe that Silicon Valley North (Ottawa's complex of computer industries) gives them high status in informatic development. In both countries, high-tech companies that lost a bundle in Wall Street's dot-com disaster see RMA as a lever for government business and the opportunity to recoup their fortunes. Given the Pentagon's commitment to transformation for each of the four American services, Canada's maritime, land and air forces will try to fit into whatever form RMA takes in their US-counterpart service. Since interoperability already governs CF capital planning, RMA merely adds focus. Ottawa has budgeted $480 million for an Omnibus Canadian Military Satellite Communications Project (CANMILSATCOM to its friends).

Canadian navy frigates, already integrated in US carrier escort groups, have to be compatible with American communications and weapons technology. To replace its two aging fleet replenishment ships, the navy is campaigning for a $2.3 billion Afloat Logistics Sealift Capability (ALSC) project to supply an onshore task force and provide limited sealift for troops and heavy equipment. A $1.226 billion Incremental Modernization Program (IMP) is bringing as many CF-18s as the air force can afford up to current US standards. Canada spent $15 million to have a stake in the new

US Joint Strike Fighter, and it has converted one of its new Airbus CC-150s as an air-to-air refuelling tanker. To provide strategic airlift, the defence department explored buying six huge Boeing C-17s. Since they would have spent most of their time on the ground, one way to cut operating costs was to loan them back to the US. However, the deal came unstuck under the weight of such complications as whose colours the aircraft would wear, which country would provide the crew, and what would happen if the US used them in a war with Cuba.

After the DND endured the same light tank–heavy tank debate that had split the US Army, Canadian land forces commander Lieutenant General Mike Jeffries lined up with General Eric Shinseki, his US counterpart. National Defence ordered 651 more light armoured vehicles (LAVs) from General Motors, to use as light armoured personnel carriers. Jeffries shifted all his tanks and other heavy combat equipment to Camp Wainwright in Alberta and dedicated the other two land-forces brigades to light or medium roles.

Historians can only get a grip on the future if they understand deep continuities. People are people: they don't change overnight, even if they think they do. Throughout their history, Canadians have depended for their security on the French, the British and, since 1945, the Americans. Why be ashamed? Our imperial partners have also acted entirely in their own self-interest and they have quit—in 1763, 1871 or whenever—the instant it no longer seemed to be in their interest. The American partnership allows Washington negotiated access to Canada's vast terrain to enhance American security. It compels Canada to do all it can not to be a danger to its neighbour. Would a bigger military effort by Ottawa give

Canada more leverage to influence US national security and defence policy? The evidence is missing. Like other sovereign countries, and more than most, the United States serves its own interests.

David L. King, a retired Canadian colonel and a faculty member at the US National Defence University in Washington, sums up Canada's military forces as irrelevant to his current employers:

> The assertion that the Canadian Forces are militarily irrelevant to the US doubtless will trouble some people, particularly within Canada's Department of National Defence (DND). However the lack of "military" relevance from a US perspective is also increasingly applicable to the rest of the United States' allies. It will startle few serious analysts to learn that no allied forces are critical to US military policy. Even a cursory read of the *American National Security Strategy*, the *National Military Strategy*, and the *Quadrennial Defense Review (QDR)* reveal that these documents take no cognizance of allied military forces. All the references to allies are in the context of the US aiding and assisting its allies, not the reverse.[10]

Americans can still give advice and reflect their resentment that the ninth biggest economy in the world spends so little on defence (or on US military contractors), but Colonel King suggests that we would have to spend enormous sums on

---

10. David L. King, "We need a Romanow Commission for Defence and Foreign Policy," *Policy Options Politiques*, vol. 23, no. 3, April 2002.

defence—six percent of our GDP or about fifty-four billion dollars a year for ten years—to create a military machine worthy of US attention—and even then, possibly, only if Canada achieved an Argentina-like state of national economic collapse. For comparison, consider that even the adoption of the Conservatives' 1987 Cold War white paper would have cost about three percent of GDP. Half that amount would put Canada's defence spending on a par with Germany and ahead of Spain and Belgium.

"Gouverner, c'est choisir," declared Pierre Mendès-France, one of the wisest of France's post-war politicians. To avoid stalling, or even burying, many current defence desires, in 2003 the federal government would have had to devote ten billion dollars—four billion more than its entire projected surplus—to defence alone. Ottawa faces powerful demands from farmers, mayors, provincial premiers, the sick and the very rich, as well military lobbyists with their peremptory commands and American-inspired appetites.

Any Liberal defence minister may find it easier to sell his colleagues and caucus on better living conditions for troops and their families than on new weapons and contracts for the defence industry. Critics of RMA and interoperability will add their own arguments: Canada has become so tied to the American defence machine that it has damaged its sovereignty, especially in the eyes of Europeans and the Third World. Electronic wizardry did not prevent the USS *Vincennes* from mistakenly destroying an Iranian civilian airliner in 1988. What if next time the rocket is US-activated, but is fired from a Canadian warship? Canada's "friendly fire" losses outside Kandahar in February 2002 are a poignant reminder of high-tech warfare's imperfections. Centralized US command, control, computers and communications erode the autonomy Canada had come to expect for its field commanders since 1918. The US model much prefers complete subordination and integration. So would you, if you commanded a high-tech allied force.

Canadians boast of their politeness and worry about the apparent rudeness of ignoring advice from President Bush's ambassador or stressing Canadian differences with his boss. Canadians *should* be polite and thoughtful—and realistic. The Americans did not order Canadian warships, aircraft or an infantry battalion to support their forces in Afghanistan; they accepted them among many allied contributions, treated them respectfully, supplied a good many of their needs from their own resources, allowed Canada a share in investigating the tragic accident that befell its troops, and offered graceful thanks at the end of their service. What ally has done better? Were we so mercenary as to expect soft-wood lumber sales as a reward?

Interoperability and RMA technologies do not disable Canadian Forces for the peace support operations (PSOs) that Canadian public opinion favours. On the contrary, invest-ments in sealift and airlift, better communications, precision-guided munitions and lighter but robust military vehicles are precisely what PSOs needed in the past and will need in the future. If close links with the United States are incompatible with UN peacekeeping or peacemaking, the Canadian armed forces would have been equally unacceptable since the Ogdensburg Agreement of 1940: neither interoperability nor US support for most PSOs began yesterday.

Peace advocates have proposed some alternative futures for Canada's armed forces. The Council of 21 proposed an international peacekeeping constabulary. Others would transform Canada's forces into a semi-trained, lightly equipped local force, capable of suppressing internal disorder. In such a form, Canada's armed forces would resemble military organizations in many Latin American, African and Asian countries and on the fringes of the former Soviet Union. Too poor to own modern weapons and equipment and sometimes even to feed their troops, many countries know that their defenders will prey on the population, terrify politicians and exploit national pride. Very few Canadians want or expect their defenders to fall into that league.

Instead, Canadians want their country to play a modest, responsible and constructive role in a sometimes dangerous and often cruel world. Given the political differences between the Chrétien and Bush administrations, the state of Canada's security and defence systems, and enormous Canadian dependence on US markets, the post–September 11 experience was a successful test of the Canada–United States relationship. Critics, especially politicians and historians, will do their best to find flaws and failure in this record. The rest of us know better.

Canadians will live in the future much as they have lived in the past—day by day. They will turn reluctantly to questions of military significance, suspicious of people who cry "wolf," and largely immune from memories of military disaster and loss. Living next to the world's only superpower is not as safe as living next to the old, pre-1940 United States. Canadians realize from walking their own multicultural streets that the world is now a very small place. We can fly from Montreal to Beijing or back again—halfway around the world—in twelve hours, without even changing our watches.

Our little corner of the world looks very attractive to people who believe they are condemned to poverty and early death by the dictates of multinational corporations and financial institutions or by the incompetent, corrupt and tyrannical regimes of their own countries.

This book has been intended to help Canadians understand some key choices for our country. Canadians can imagine themselves to be anywhere in the world, but they usually wake up here, with the same neighbours, the same problems and a little less time to do whatever needs doing. If you have read this far, your understanding of some major Canadian defence issues has taken a big step forward. If the choices now look more complex than they did, welcome to reality.

Glossary

ABM: Anti-ballistic missile

ALSC: Afloat Logistics Sealift Capability

AWACS: Airborne Warning and Control System

BC: British Columbia

BCATP: British Commonwealth Air Training Plan

BIC: Battle Information Centre

BNA Act: British North America Act

C4IST: Command, control, computers, communication, intelligence, surveillance and targeting

CCCRH: The Canadian Committee for the Control of Radiation Hazards

CCF: Co-operative Commonwealth Federation

CCOS: Chief of the Chiefs of Staff Committee

CDS: Chief of the Defence Staff

CEF: Canadian Expeditionary Force

CENCOM: Central Command

CF: Canadian Forces

CFB: Canadian Forces Base

CFE: Canadian Forces Europe

CFHQ: Canadian Forces Headquarters

CGS: Chief of the General Staff

CIA: Central Intelligence Agency (US)

COs: Conscientious objectors

CPC: Communist Party of Canada

CPPNW: Canadian Physicians for the Prevention of Nuclear War

CSIS: Canadian Security and Intelligence Service

CUCND: Combined Universities Campaign for Nuclear Disarmament

DEW Line: Distant Early Warning Radar Line

DND: Department of National Defence

FLUs: French-Language Units

FOR: Fellowship of Reconciliation

GPS: Global positioning system

HMCS: Her Majesty's Canadian Ship

ICBM: Intercontinental ballistic missile

IDF: Israel Defence Forces

IRA: Irish Republican Army

IRBM: Intermediate range ballistic missile

JSF: Joint Strike Fighter

JTRS [or "Jitters"]: Joint tactical radio system

LAV: Light armoured vehicle

LMF: Lack of moral fibre

MISC: The McGill Institute for the Study of Canada

MOC: Military Occupational Category

MP: Member of Parliament

MSA: Military Service Act (conscription, 1917)

NATO: The North Atlantic Treaty Organization

NCM: Non-commissioned Member

NCO: Non-commissioned Officer

NDHQ: National Defence Headquarters

NGO: Non-governmental organization

NORAD: North American Aerospace Command (*originally* North American Air Defence Command)

NORCOM: Northern Command

NPAM: Non-permanent Active Militia

NRMA: National Resources Mobilization Act (conscription, 1940)

NRMA men: Home-service conscripts, rudely called "zombies"

OLQs: Officer-like qualities

OSI: Operational stress injury

OSOMM: Organization of Spouses of Military Members

PEI: Prince Edward Island

PF: Permanent Force

PGM: Precision-guided missiles (*or* munitions)

PJBD: Permanent Joint Board of Defence

PLA: People's Liberation Army (China)

Plan Red: The American Army's plan for war with Great Britain

PPCLI: Princess Patricia's Canadian Light Infantry

PRC: People's Republic of China

PSO: Peace support operation

PTSD: Post-traumatic stress disorder

PW: Prisoner of war

QDR: Quadrennial Defense Review (US)

R22eR: Royal 22e Régiment

RAF: Royal Air Force

RCAF: Royal Canadian Air Force

RCMP: Royal Canadian Mounted Police

RCN: Royal Canadian Navy

RCR: Royal Canadian Regiment

RMA: Revolution in Military Affairs

RMC: Royal Military College of Canada

RN: Royal Navy

SAM: Surface-to-air missile

SAR: Search and rescue

SOP: Standard operating procedure

SSM: Surface-to-surface missile

TNT: Trinitrotoluene (an explosive)

UCAV: Unmanned combat air vehicle

UAV: Unmanned air vehicle

UN: United Nations

USMA: United States Military Academy

USS: United States Ship

USSR: Union of Soviet Socialist Republics

VANW: Veterans Against Nuclear War

VC: Victoria Cross

VOW: Voice of Women

WO: Warrant Officer

WPTB: Wartime Prices and Trade Board

Selected Readings

For an allegedly unmilitary people, Canadians have a strong appetite for military history and a persistent interest in the dilemmas of their own defence. Much as the CBC was a balanced answer to the early broadcasting dilemma of "the State or the States," official history has provided a respected and often critical core of understanding, but veterans, critics, academic scholars and thoughtful citizens have also given Canadians plenty to read. This list is a tiny sample of what a Canadian military library could contain. It is drawn from the books I think my students at McGill and the University of Toronto needed to enlarge their understanding of Canada's defence. I know that the list never stops growing.

General

Dewitt, David B. and David Leyton-Brown (eds.), *Canada's International Security Policy* (Toronto, 1995)

German, Tony, *The Sea Is at Our Gates: The History of the Canadian Navy* (Toronto, 1990)

Granatstein, J. L., *Canada's Army: Waging War and Keeping the Peace* (Toronto, 2002)

———— and Norman Hillmer, *Empire to Umpire: Canada and the World to the 1990s* (Toronto, 1994)

Milberry, Larry, *Sixty Years: The RCAF and the CF Air Command, 1924–1984* (Toronto, 1988)

Milner, Marc, *Canada's Navy: The First Century* (Toronto, 1999)

Morton, Desmond, *A Military History of Canada: From Champlain to Kosovo* (Toronto, 1999)

Stacey, C. P., *A Date with History: Memoirs of a Canadian Historian* (Toronto, 1987)

1763–1914

Harris, Stephen, *Canadian Brass: The Making of a Professional Army* (Toronto, 1988)

Hitsman, J. Mackay, *Safeguarding Canada, 1763–1871* (Toronto, 1968)

Miller, Carman, *Painting the Map Red: Canada and the South African War, 1899–1902* (Montreal, 1993)

Morton, Desmond, *The Canadian General: Sir William Otter* (Toronto, 1974)

Preston, R. A., *Canada and "Imperial Defense": A Study of the Origins of the British Commonwealth Defense Organization, 1867–1919* (Toronto & Durham, 1967)

Stacey, C. P., *Canada and the British Army: A Study in the Practice of Responsible Government, 1846–1871* (London, 1936; Toronto, 1963)

1914–1939

Armstrong, Elizabeth, *The Crisis of Quebec, 1914–1918* (New York, 1967; Toronto, 1974)

Bird, W. R., *As We Go On* (Toronto, 1930) or *Ghosts Have Warm Hands* (Toronto, 1960)

Dancocks, Daniel, *Welcome to Flanders Fields: The First Canadian Battle of the Great War: Ypres, 1915* (Toronto, 1988)

Eayrs, James, *In Defence of Canada*, vols. I–II (Toronto, 1964, 1966)

Morton, Desmond, *When Your Number's Up: The Canadian Soldier in the First World War* (Toronto, 1993)

———— and J. L. Granatstein, *Marching to Armageddon: Canadians and the Great War, 1914–1919* (Toronto, 1989)

Rawling, Bill, *Surviving Trench Warfare: Technology and the Canadian Corps* (Toronto, 1992)

Roy, R. H. (ed.), *The Journal of Private Fraser, 1914–1918, Canadian Expeditionary Force* (Victoria, 1985)

Vance, Jonathan, *Death So Noble: Memory, Meaning and the First World War* (Vancouver, 1997)

1939–1945

Copp, Terry and William MacAndrew, *Battle Exhaustion: Soldiers and Psychiatrists in the Canadian Army, 1939–1945* (Montreal, 1990)

English, John A., *The Canadian Army and the Normandy Campaign: A Study of Failure in High Command* (New York, 1991)

Granatstein, J. L. *The Generals: The Canadian Army's Senior Commanders in the Second World War* (Don Mills, 1993)

—— and Desmond Morton, *Forged in Fire: Canadians and the Second World War, 1939–1945* (Toronto, 1990)

Lawrence, Hal, *A Bloody War: One Man's Memories of the Canadian Navy, 1939–45* (Toronto, 1979)

Milner, Marc, *North Atlantic Run: The Royal Canadian Navy and the Battle of the Convoys* (Toronto, 1985)

Mowat, Farley, *The Regiment* (Toronto, 1955)

Peden, Murray, *A Thousand Shall Fall* (Stittsville, 1981)

Zimmerman, David, *The Great Naval Battle of Ottawa* (Toronto, 1989)

1945–1968

Allard, Jean-Victor, *The Memoirs of General Jean-V. Allard* (Vancouver, 1988)

Burns, E. L. M., *Between Arab and Israeli* (Toronto, 1962)

Hellyer, Paul, *Damn the Torpedoes: My Fight to Unify Canada's Armed Forces* (Toronto, 1990)

Jockel, Joseph T. *No Boundaries Upstairs: Canada, the United States, and the Origins of North American Air Defence, 1945–1958* (Vancouver, 1987)

1968–2003

Bercuson, David, *Significant Incident: Canada's Army, The Airborne, and the Murder in Somalia* (Toronto, 1996)

Bland, Douglas, *Chiefs of Defence: Government and the Unified Command of the Canadian Armed Forces* (Toronto, 1995)

Code, David E. and Ian Cameron, *Canadian Forces and the Modern World* (Ottawa, 1993)

Cuthbertson, Brian, *Canadian Military Independence in the Age of the Superpowers* (Toronto, 1977)

Davis, James R., *The Sharp End: A Canadian Soldier's Story* (Vancouver, 1997)

Harrison, Deborah and Lucie Laliberté, *No Life Like It: Military Wives in Canada* (Toronto, 1994)

Ignatieff, Michael, *The Warrior's Honour: Ethnic War and Modern Conscience* (Toronto, 1999)

Mackenzie, Lewis, *Peacekeeper: The Road to Sarajevo* (Toronto, 1993)

Morrison, Alex, *Peacekeeping, Peacemaking or War: International Security Enforcement* (Toronto, 1991)

Pope, W. H., *Leading From the Front: The War Memoirs of Harry Pope* (Waterloo, 2002).

Sloan, Elinor C., *The Revolution in Military Affairs* (Montreal & Kingston, 2002)

Sokolsky, Joel, *Defending Canada: U.S.–Canadian Defense Policies* (New York, 1989)

Official Histories

Douglas, W. A. B., *The Creation of a National Air Force: The Official History of the Royal Canadian Air Force,* vol. II (Ottawa, 1986)

Gimblett, Richard and Jean Morin, *Operation Friction: Canadian Forces in the Gulf War* (Toronto, 1996)

Greenhous, Brereton, *The Crucible of War, 1939–1945: The Official History of the Royal Canadian Air Force*, vol. III (Toronto, 1994)

Nicholson, G. W. L., *The Official History of the Canadian Army in the First World War: Canadian Expeditionary Force, 1914–1919* (Ottawa, 1962)

———, *The Official History of the Canadian Army in the Second World War: The Canadians in Italy, 1943–1945* (Ottawa, 1957)

Schull, Joseph, *The Far Distant Ships: An Official Account of Canadian Naval Operations in the Second World War* (Ottawa, 1952)

Stacey, C. P. *The Official History of the Canadian Army in the Second World War: Six Years of War: The Canadian Army in Canada, Britain and the Pacific* (Ottawa, 1955)

———, *The Victory Campaign: Operations in North-West Europe, 1944–1945* (Ottawa, 1958)

———, *Arms, Men and Governments: The War Policies of Canada, 1939–1945* (Ottawa, 1970)

Tucker, G. N., *The Naval Service of Canada: Its Official History* (2 vols.) (Ottawa, 1962)

Wise, S. F., *Canadian Airmen and the First World War: The Official History of the Royal Canadian Air Force*, vol. I (Toronto, 1980)

Wood, Herbert F., *Strange Battleground: The Operations in Korea and Their Effects on the Defence Policy of Canada* (Ottawa, 1966)

Index

A

Abbreviations/acronyms, 214–218
Aberdeen, Lady, 105
ABM treaty, 82n
Aboriginal burial grounds, 28
Afghanistan War, 22, 201n, 203, 204
Afloat Logistics Sealift Capability (ALSC), 207
Aitken, Max (Lord Beaverbrook), 54
Alaska Highway, 96
Alfred, Taiaiake, 127n
Allard, Jean-Victor, 182
ALSC, 207
Armed forces. *See* Canadian Forces (CF)
Arnold, Benedict, 30n
Arone, Shidane, 89, 90
Aronson's XVIth Law, 143n
Arsenal, 201
Asselin, Olivar, 44n
Asymmetric warfare, 20–21, 198
Atkinson, Joe, 106, 107
Atomic bomb, 113
Attlee, Clement, 77

B

Avro Arrow, 75, 176–177, 191
Axworthy, Tom, 90

Ballistic Missiles Early Warning System (BMEWS), 83
Bandit, 93n
Baril, Maurice, 91, 129, 206
Barker, W. G., 50
Battle exhaustion, 126
Battle Exhaustion: Soldiers and Psychiatrists in the Canadian Army (Copp/McAndrew), 124n
Battle Information Centre (BIC), 196
Battle of Paardeberg, 38
Battle of the Marne, 197
Battle of the Somme, 48
BCATP, 56, 172
Beatty, Perrin, 85, 187
Beaverbrook, Lord, 54
Bennett, R. B., 54, 108n
Bercuson, David, 193n
Berlin Wall, 86, 116, 118
Bethune, Norman, 111
BIC, 196

Big Cut, 54
Biggar, O. M., 96
Bishop, Billy, 28, 50
Black hats, 186
Black Watch, 28, 46
Bloody Sunday (Jan 30/72), 198
BMEWS, 83
Boer War, 38–39, 106
Bomarc, 75, 178
Borden, Fred, 36, 40, 141, 166
Borden, Harold, 40n
Borden, Sir Robert Laird, 41, 44, 45, 49, 52, 56, 167, 178
Bourassa, Henri, 38, 41
Bowell, Mackenzie, 165
British Commonwealth Air Training Plan (BCATP), 56, 172
Brock, Isaac, 30
Burns, E. L. M. "Smiling Sunray," 60
Bush, George H. W., 22, 87, 88, 120, 203
Byng, Sir Julian, 49

C

Campbell, Kim, 89, 90
Canadian-American defence partnership, 13. See also Ogdensburg Agreement
Canadian-American International Joint Commission, 107
Canadian Army and the Normandy Campaign: A Study of Failure in High Command, The (English), 171
Canadian Defence League, 40, 44, 107
Canadian Expeditionary Force (CEF), 46
Canadian Forces (CF), 122–146
  age of troops, 150–151
  basic training, 125–127
  civil authority, 157–158
  civilianization, 143, 184–185
  class system, 137–143
  Cold War, 136, 173
  disciplines, 158–161
  domestic role, 15–16
  ethical ways of fighting, 129–130
  family life, 151–156
  future developments, 190–213
  halycon times, 175
  leadership, 162–189
  NCOs, 137–139
  psychological problems, 124
  rank-bloat, 143
  reservists, 72n, 135–137
  spouses, 154–157
  uniform, 182–183
  zero tolerance, 144
Canadian Forces Europe (CFE), 183
Canadian Institute for Peace and Security, 118
Canadian Peace Alliance (CPA), 118

Canadian Physicians for the Prevention of Nuclear War (CPPNW), 118
Canadian War Museum, 25
Canadian War Records Office, 54
CANMILSATCOM, 207
Cardwell, Edward, 140
Carter, Jimmy, 83
Cartier, Sir George-Étienne, 33
Castro, Fidel, 78, 178
CCF, 108–109
Cellucci, Paul, 1–3, 24
CFE, 183
CF-18, 148, 207
CF-100 (Canuck), 69, 75
CF-105 Arrow, 75, 176
Challenge and Commitment (1989 white paper), 14, 85, 187, 192
Chateauguay, 30
China, 205–206
Chlorine gas, 47, 48
Chrétien, Jean, 17, 23, 90, 91, 120, 188, 189
Churchill, Winston, 95, 173, 178
Civilian Conservation Corps, 55n
Civilianization, 143, 184–185
Class system, 137–143
Classification creep, 143
Claxton, Brooke, 145, 174, 180, 191
Cold War, 64–86
    Avro Arrow, 75, 176–177, 191

Berlin Wall, 116
Canadian military preparedness, 13
Canadian troops, 136, 173
Cuban Missile Crisis, 78, 116, 179
first strike, second strike doctrine, 76n
Korean War, 70, 71
peace movements, 113–118
peacekeeping, 73–74
Red Square, displays of military might, 115
Collège militaire royal de St-Jean, 140
Collins, Mary, 156
Collishaw, Raymond, 50
Colombo Plan, 114
Colonel's Day, 35
Combined Universities Campaign for Nuclear Disarmament (CUCND), 115
Communist Party, 112
Condottieri, 131
Conrad Grebel College, 117
Conscientious objectors (COs), 108, 112
Copp, Moses, 30n
Cormorants, 90n
Cougar, 81
Council of 21, 17, 212
Coyote, 92n
CPA, 118
CPPNW, 118
Crerar, Harry, 59, 60, 172
Crimean War, 31
Crimson Route, 96

Cromwell, Oliver, 163
Cruikshank, Ernest, 54
Cuban Missile Crisis, 78, 116, 179
CUCND, 115
Currie, Arthur, 46n, 49
Curtis, Wilfrid, 173
C4IST, 196

D

Dallaire, Roméo, 89, 188
DeChastelain, John, 187
Defence Plan No. 1, 9, 36
Defence spending, 2, 178, 207–208
Dekanahwideh, 103
Denison, George T., 37
Desbarats, Georges, 169
DEW Line, 12, 75
Diefenbaker, John, 76, 77, 116, 176, 177, 178, 179, 180, 191
Dieppe, 59
Discipline, 158–161
Distant Early Warning (DEW) Line, 12, 75
Domestic threats, 15–16
Doukhobors, 112
Duguid, A. F., 54
Dumont, Gabriel, 36n
Dundonald, Lord, 166, 168
Dunn, James, 36

E

EH-104 helicopters, 90
Eisenhower, Dwight D., 71, 74, 77, 79, 175, 178

Emergency Act, 158
Emergency Powers Act, 72
Endicott, J. G., 114, 177
English, John, 59, 171
Ethical ways of fighting, 129–130
Ever-Victorious Corps, 139n

F

F-18-A/B Hornet, 98
F-101 Voodoo, 75
Family life, 151–156
Family Resource Centres, 156
Fellowship of Reconciliation (FOR), 110, 111n
Fenians, 32
First Anglo-Afghan war, 204n
First strike, second strike doctrine, 76n
Fisher, Sir John, 185
FOR, 110, 111n
Foucault, Michel, 20
Foulkes, Charles, 174, 175, 180
48th Highlanders, 46
Franks, Tommy, 22
Frederick the Great, 159
French, Sir John, 48
Friendly fire, death by (2002), 203, 210
Frink, Nathaniel, 30n
Future developments, 190–213

G

Generals' mutiny, 61
Generals: The Canadian Army's Senior Commanders in the

Second World War, The
(Granatstein), 144, 171n
George VI, 56
George, David Lloyd, 178
Girouard, Percy, 37
Glasnost, 86, 118
Glassco, J. Grant, 180
Gorbachev, Mikhail, 86, 118
Gordon, Charles, 37
Gouzenko, Igor, 65
Graham, Hugh, 37
Granatstein, Jack L., 144, 171
Grant, George, 177
Grant, Hugh, 173
Greenpeace, 80
Green, Howard, 115, 116, 179
Guerilla warfare, 159n
Gulf War, 43–44, 87–88, 120
Gulf War syndrome, 88n
Gwatkin, Willoughby, 167

H

Halifax Patrol, 50
Halifax Program, 167
Hall, William, 37
Harkness, Doug, 179
Harrison, Deborah, 157n
Hawkwood, Sir John, 131
Hébert, P.O. J., 37
Hellyer, Paul, 180–184
Herbert, Ivor, 166
HMCS *Bonaventure*, 184
HMCS *Rainbow*, 50
HMS *Charybdis*, 163n
Hoffmesiter, Bert, 59
Holbrooke, Richard, 202

Home-front conscription, 112
Hoodless, Adelaide, 105
Hose, Walter, 169
Howe, C. D., 58n, 72, 75
Hughes, James, 40n
Hughes, Sam, 37, 40n, 41, 42,
45, 46, 51n, 167
Hussein, Saddam, 87, 88,
203–204
Hutterites, 103
Hutton, Edward, 166

I

ICBMs, 77, 78, 115
"In Flanders' Fields," 28, 48
Incremental Modernization
Program (IMP), 207
Indian Mutiny, 31
Intercontinental ballistic missiles (ICBMs), 77, 78, 115
International Bible Students
(Jehovah's Witnesses), 108n,
112
Interoperability, 98–99

J

Jackson, Andrew, 164
Jamieson, Laura, 109
Japanese-Canadians, internment of, 62
Jeffries, Mike, 208
Jehovah's Witnesses, 108n,
112
Jervois, William F. D., 8, 32
Jockel, Joe, 3

K

Keller, Rod "Captain Blood," 60
Kennedy, John F., 78, 116, 179
Khruschev, Nikita, 78
King, David L., 209
King, William Lyon Mackenzie, 5, 23, 44, 52, 55, 56, 57, 61, 68, 70, 95, 98, 107, 109n, 110, 111, 170, 171, 172, 173, 178
Kipling, Rudyard, 138
Kiska, 62
Kissinger, Henry, 176n
Korean War, 70, 71
Kosovo, 89, 92, 202

L

LaGuardia, Fiorello, 96
Lake, Percy, 167
Laliberté, Lucie, 157n
Laurier, Sir Wilfrid, 35, 38, 39, 41, 106
Leadership, 162–189
League for Peace and Freedom, 111
Little Black Devils, 46
LMF, 160
Luard, R. G. A., 166, 168
Lundy's Lane, 30

M

MacArthur, Douglas, 71
MacBrien, J. H., 169
Macdonald, Angus L., 171
Macdonald, Donald S., 184

Macdonald, Sir John A., 8–9, 35, 164
Mackenzie King. See King, William Lyon Mackenzie
Mackenzie, Alexander, 34
Mackenzie, Colin, 167
Macphail, Agnes, 109, 112
Mahoney, Sean, 16
Masse, Marcel, 187
McCrae, John, 28
McCurdy, F. B., 41
McDonnell-Douglas CF-18, 82
McDougall, Patrick, 165
McNaughton, Andrew G. L., 9, 54, 58, 59, 61, 169, 170, 172
Megaton bomb, 74n
Mendès-France, Pierre, 210
Mennonites, 103, 112
Mercenaries, 131
Middleton, Fred, 36n, 166
Military discipline, 158–161
Military equipment, 148–150
Military ethics classes, 129–130
Military families, 151–156
Military life. See Canadian Forces (CF)
Military museums, 25–27
Military occupational category (MOC), 124
Military Service Act (MSA), 51, 104, 108n
Military spouses, 154–157
Militia, 77, 137
Militia Act, 33, 103
Miller, Frank, 180, 182

Milosevic, Slobodan, 202, 204
Minto, Lord, 38
MOC, 124
Mohawks, 127n
Monk, Henry Wentworth, 104
Montcalm, Marquis de, 29
Montgomery, Bernard, 175n
Moskos, Charles, 154
Mulroney, Brian, 13, 14, 84, 88, 90, 120, 192
Munich Agreement, 55
Murray, L. W., 57, 171
Mussolini, 11

N

Napoleon, 151
National Defence College, 69, 91, 145
National Defence Headquarters (NDHQ), 146
National Resources Mobilization Act (NRMA), 57
Nationalistes, 41
NATO, 68, 114-115
NCOs, 137–139
NDHQ, 146
Niebuhr, Reinhold, 110
Nixon, Richard, 82
Non-commissioned officers (NCOs), 137–139
NORAD, 12, 76
Nordheimer, Edith Boulton, 106
Norstad, Lauris, 179
North American *Aerospace* Defence Command, 12–13

North American Defence Command (NORAD), 12, 76
North Atlantic Treaty Organization (NATO), 68, 114-115
NRMA men, 61, 62, 170
Nursing, 141

O

October Crisis, 80
Ogdensburg Agreement, 5, 11, 67, 95
Olgarkov, Nikolai, 194
Omnibus Canadian Military Satellite Communications Project (CANMILSAT-COM), 207
Omniplex, 125
Operation Dismantle, 117
Operation ESSAY, 80
Operational stress injuries (OSI), 124
Oppenheimer, Robert, 113
OSOMM (Organization of Spouses of Military Members), 157n
Otter, William, 38, 167

P

Patriotic Fund, 154
Peace movements, 102–121
    Cold War, 113–118
    farmers, 105
    FOR, 110, 110n
    Operation Dismantle, 117

peacekeeping, 119
religious pacifism, 103
secular pacifism, 104
women, 105
WWI, 112
WWII, 113
Peace of Paris, 7
Peacekeeping, 16–17, 73–74
    Congo, 17, 73
    Cyprus, 17, 73
    Eritrea, 92–93
    Kashmir, 16, 73
    Kosovo, 89
    peace movement, 119
    Suez Canal, 16–17, 73
Pearkes, George, 176, 178
Pearson, Lester B., 73, 116, 117, 180
Perestroika, 86, 118
Permanent Force (PF), 35, 42, 53, 69
Perry, Aylesworth Bowen, 37n
PGMs, 202
Picasso, Pablo, 114
Pinetree Line, 75
Plan Red, 9
Platforms, 199
Plymouth Brethren, 108n
Pope, Maurice, 172–173
Post-traumatic stress disorder (PTSD), 124, 126
Powell, Walker, 165
Precision-guided missiles (PGMs), 202
Predator UCAV, 201n
Price, William, 45

Princess Patricia's Canadian Light Infantry (PPCLI), 53
Project Ploughshares, 117
Psychological problems, 124
PTSD, 124, 126

Q

Quakers, 103, 112
Quebec Act, 29

R

Ralston, J. L., 61, 169, 170
Rank-bloat, 143
RCNR, 136n
RCNVR, 136n
Reagan, Ronald, 83, 117, 118, 192, 194
Red Square, displays of military might, 115
Reference books, 219–224
Régiment Carignan-Salières, 133
Relief camps, 55n
Religious pacifism, 103
Renan, Ernest, 49
Reserve militia, 33n
Reservists, 72n, 135–137
Riel, Louis, 36
RMA, 195–207
Robertson, Norman, 116
Roberts, Sir Frederick, 204
Rogers, Robert, 28
Roosevelt, Franklin Delano, 5, 11, 173, 178
Ross rifle, 42, 46

Royal Canadian Navy Reserve (RCNR), 136n
Royal Canadian Navy Volunteer Reserve (RCNVR), 136n
Royal Military College of Canada, 34, 128, 140
Royal Twenty-Centers, 55n
Rumsfeld, Donald, 201
Rwanda (Hutu-Tutsi civil war), 89

S

"S" (stability factor), 124
Salaberry, Charles de, 30
Salisbury Plain, 46
SAM, 83n
Schmidt, Helmut, 81, 186
Scott, Richard, 106
Search-and-rescue helicopters, 90n
Second Ypres, 47
Segal, Mady, 151
Selby-Smyth, Sir Edward, 165
September 11 terrorist attacks, 21, 93–94
Seward, William, 32
Shaping the Future of Canadian Defence: A Strategy for 2020, 206
Shinseki, Eric, 199, 208
Simcoe, John, 30, 164
Simonds, Guy, 59, 142, 174, 175, 181
Smith, Goldwyn, 106
Smythe, Conn, 61

Sokolsky, Joel, 3
Somalia affair, 89–90
Somalia inquiry, 17, 91, 129
Spouses, 154–157
Sputnik, 76, 115
SS-20s, 83
Stalin, Josef, 100
Stein, Janice, 90
Stoppages, 152n
Strategic Defence Initiative, 83
St. Laurent, Louis, 70, 71, 97
Suggested readings, 219–224
Sutherland, R. J., 76n

T

Thirty Years War, 132
Thomas, Charles, 90, 187
Tilley, Sir Leonard, 97n
Tobin, Brian, 18
Trafalgar (1805), 143
Treaty of Washington, 8, 33
Trench warfare, 139n
Troops. *See* Canadian Forces (CF)
Trudeau, Pierre Elliott, 13, 79, 80, 81, 83, 84, 118, 125, 126, 183, 184, 186, 187
Truman, Harry, 68, 77, 178
Turbot War, 18
Turner, John, 84

U

Uniform, 182–183
Unmanned air vehicles (UAVs), 201n

Unmanned combat air vehicles (UCAVs), 201n
USS *Vincennes*, 210
U.S.S.R., collapse of, 86, 118

V

Valcartier, 45
Van Doos, 51n, 53
Vegetius, 158
Versailles, 49
Veterans Against Nuclear War (VANW), 118
Vietnam War, 79
Vimy Ridge, 48, 139n
Voice of Women (VOW), 115, 177

W

War Measures Act, 15n, 158
War of 1812, 7n, 30, 31
Warrant officers (WOs), 138
Wavy Navy, 136n
Wellington, Duke of, 151
White paper
1949, 70, 191
1964, 191

1987, 14, 85, 187, 192
1994, 192
WIL, 109
Winters, Dennis, 141
Wolfe, James, 29
Women's International League for Peace and Freedom (WIL), 109
Woodsworth, James Shaver, 108, 111, 112
Woodsworth, Lucy, 109
World War I, 44–52, 95
World War II, 55–63, 95, 170
Wotton, Sir Henry, 4

Y

Yeoman, Letitia, 105
Yonge, George, 164
Young, Douglas, 18, 91, 145
Ypres, 47
Yugoslavia, breakup of, 89

Z

Zero tolerance, 92, 144
Zombies, 60